C000183789

THE GOSPEL
AS TAUGHT BY CALVIN

JOHANNES CALVINUS.

NATUS X.IUL.MDIX.

OBIIT XXVII.MAI.MDLXIV.

PROMPTE ET SINCERE IN OPERE DOMINI

THE GOSPEL
AS TAUGHT BY CALVIN

R. C. Reed

*We forget to speak well when
we cease to speak with God.*
John Calvin

THE BANNER OF TRUTH TRUST

THE BANNER OF TRUTH TRUST
3 Murrayfield Road, Edinburgh EH12 6EL, UK
P.O. Box 621, Carlisle, PA 17013, USA

First published by
The Presbyterian Reformation Society,
Jackson, Mississippi

*

First Banner of Truth edition 2009

*

ISBN-13: 978 1 84871 030 6

Typeset in 11/15 pt Sabon Oldstyle Figures at
the Banner of Truth Trust
Printed in the U.S.A. by
Versa Press, Inc.,
East Peoria, IL

CONTENTS

Foreword *vii*

Preface *xi*

1. An Historic Glance 1

2. Point 1 — The Fatal Image 15

3. Point 2 — An Opened Heart 33

4. Point 3 — First Choice 47

5. Point 4 — Boundary Lines 69

6. Point 5 — Grace Linked to Glory 83

7. Calvinism Tested by Love 99

8. Calvinism Tested by Fruit 123

FOREWORD

*D*r R. C. Reed was born in Hamilton County, Tennessee in 1851. He was educated at King College and Union Theological Seminary (Virginia). He served a number of pastorates, including the Woodland Street Church of Nashville mentioned in the dedication. It was from this Church that he was called in 1898 to be Professor of Ecclesiastical History and Church Polity at Columbia Theological Seminary (then at Columbia, South Carolina). He continued in this capacity until his death in 1925.

Dr Reed was a much loved pastor and professor. He united in himself both a kind gentleness and a strong conviction of faith. Being fully committed to the historic position of his Presbyterian heritage, he wrote this little booklet to assist others to come to this same faith. In addition to this work, he authored several other books, the most significant being: *History of the Presbyterian Churches of the World* and *What is the Kingdom of God?*

In republishing this little book, it is the hope of the editors that God may use it to help many of his little ones to come to a better understanding of the gospel of grace.

Morton H. Smith

To
the Members of
Woodland Street Presbyterian Church,
Whose Loving Appreciation
Has Been
a Constant Stimulus
to Earnest Efforts for Their Good,
This Little Book
Is Affectionately Dedicated
by the Author.

PREFACE

*T*his is not an age of doctrinal controversy. In this fact we rejoice. The evangelical churches are much better employed than they would be in wrangling over doctrinal differences. They can accomplish far more good by uniting their forces to fight a common enemy than by training their guns at each other and leaving the devil to look on as a delighted spectator.

This does not mean that there should be no exposition of those doctrines which furnish ground for denominational divisions. These doctrines are not essential to salvation, and should not monopolize attention. Many of them are important, and should not be ignored. 'All Scripture is given by inspiration of God, and is profitable' (2 *Tim.* 3:16). Some doctrines for which the Presbyterian Church stands are among the 'hard things to be understood' of which 'our beloved brother, Paul, wrote' (cf. 2 *Pet.* 3:15-16). But they were written for our learning, and must not be suppressed.

Calvin, whose name we delight to honour, has wisely admonished us not to keep back what God designed to make known.

> The Scripture is the school of the Holy Ghost, in which, as nothing necessary and useful to be known is omitted, so nothing is taught which it is not beneficial to know. Whatever, therefore, is declared in the Scripture concerning predestination we must be cautious not to withhold from the faithful, lest we appear either to defraud them of the favour of God or to reprove and censure the Holy Spirit for publishing what it would be useful by any means to suppress. Let us, I say, permit the Christian man to open his heart and his ears to all the discourses addressed to him by God, only with this moderation, that as soon as the Lord closes his sacred mouth, he shall also desist from further inquiry. This will be the best barrier of sobriety, if, in learning, we not only follow the leadings of God, but as soon as he ceases to teach, we give up our desire of learning.

In our modest attempt to expound the high doctrines which are inseparably associated with the name of this illustrious man, we shall endeavour to heed his judicious caution.

R. C. R.

THE GOSPEL
AS TAUGHT BY CALVIN

1

AN HISTORIC GLANCE

*P*resbyterianism has ever laid the supreme stress on doctrine. It does not magnify matters of ritual nor points of order. Its contention with other churches is mainly over the doctrines of sin and salvation, not over forms of worship or the mere externals of religious profession. It has expended an immense amount of energy in formulating, propagating and defending a certain system of belief. It is today the champion of an elaborate creed, publishing to the world its deeply settled convictions on all the great problems of man's spiritual history, condition and destiny. It has not yielded to the popular clamour against dogma. It finds in dogma the divine incentive to duty, and can no more dispense with the one than disparage the other. It is not afraid to say what it believes in terms as strong and plain as the language of the Bible. It makes no boast of progress, so far as it relates to doctrinal development. It built at first on the Rock. Sand shifts; rock is permanent. It stands today on Reformation theology. Reformation theology represented a progress backward. The Presbyterian Church believes that all true progress in theology lies in the direction of the Divine Teacher and his apostles. The goal is behind us.

At present two great systems of theology divide the Christian world—Calvinism and Arminianism. These stand out as bold mountain ranges; and all other phases of theological thought that are worthy of notice are but foothills or spurs belonging to one or other of these ranges. These two systems, starting from premises that lie close together, diverge more and more as they develop, and in the end are logically poles apart. It is popularly supposed that Calvinism stands for divine sovereignty, and Arminianism for human freedom; but neither system denies the postulate of the other. The difference is one of emphasis. Calvinism, while asserting the freedom of man, writes divine sovereignty in large capitals. Arminianism, while admitting the sovereignty of God, writes human freedom in large capitals. If this were the only difference, or the main difference, between these two great rival systems, it would matter little which prevailed. But they are based on radically different philosophies of human life. True, each claims as its lowest basis the word of God, but inevitably the interpretation put on the word will be coloured by the accepted philosophy.

It is our purpose to expound Calvinism; but this can best be done by noting its contrast with opposing views. It will, therefore, form a fit introduction to take a brief glance at the historic origin of these two great rival systems.

I. Whence the Name Calvinism?

From John Calvin, of course; but we should greatly err if we supposed the thing designated by this name originated with Calvin. It never occurred to him to set forth an original system of theology. He did merely what Luther and Melanchthon and Zwingli did: he preached and taught the doctrines of grace in order to reform the church and overthrow the papacy. All these reformers found such doctrines strongly set forth by the great church father, Augustine, a man whom the papacy had canonized. In preaching these doctrines, as a war measure, they made much use of the name of Augustine. They were thus turning the biggest gun of Roman Catholicism against itself. Hence, Reformation theology was little more than revived Augustinianism. It so happened that, among the mighty ones who aided in this revival, Calvin was in certain respects the mightiest. He was the most profound thinker and the wisest organizer. He was also a great scholar and a voluminous writer. He thoroughly gleaned the works of Augustine, separated the gold from the dross, added something from his own mint, and gave the priceless treasure to the world.

We recognize neither Calvin nor Augustine as the author of that system of truth for which the Presbyterian Church stands. At the same time, we are not ashamed of the association of their names with our church. From Paul to Calvin there arose not a greater than Augustine; from Paul to our day there has not arisen a greater than John Calvin. He began his education with a view to the priesthood of Rome. By his father's advice he turned aside to law. His career was most brilliant. While still a law student, at the age of twenty, he gave lectures to the class in the absence of the professor, and was honoured, when hardly more than a boy in years, with the complimentary title of Doctor of Laws. At twenty-three he was converted, and four years later he issued the first edition of his *Institutes of the Christian Religion*—a work destined to exercise a wider and a more permanent influence on the thought of the world than any other theological treatise ever written. In his twenty-seventh year he went to Geneva, not intending to make that his home, but was induced to remain by the solemn admonitions of his fellow countryman, William Farel. Before two years were ended, both Farel and Calvin were deposed from the ministry and expelled from the city, because of their efforts at reform and the severity of discipline which they tried to enforce.

Calvin was soon recalled, and from then till the day of his death he was almost an absolute autocrat of the little republic of Geneva. He was such, however, solely by the masterful power of his intellect and the force of his character. What was the result? In a little while Geneva was radiant with the glory of a purified church and a reformed municipality. Calvin's fame spread far and wide, and students by the thousand flocked to Geneva to attend his lectures, and many who were oppressed by tyranny elsewhere sought a place of safety under the sway of his influence.

Let it not be imagined, however, that our church regards Calvin as having been either infallible or impeccable. It has not blindly followed his lead. It has discarded some of his teachings as erroneous, and deplored some of his acts as wrong. But it must be remembered that he was born when the shadows of spiritual and intellectual night, which had rested in such dense folds on Europe for centuries, were just beginning to recede. The wonder is not that he failed to see all the truth, but that he saw so much; the wonder is not that he failed to free himself from all the fetters forged by the spirit of the age in which he lived, but that he attained unto so large a measure of liberty. Notwithstanding some errors of thought and some mistakes of conduct, we may safely say that God has blessed the world with few greater intellects or nobler characters than John Calvin. He has never had a detractor who could measure up to the level of his shoulder. When the multitudes who ignorantly caricature the system of truth which he taught, and try, by abuse, to tarnish the glory of his name, have been forgotten, his fame will shine on in its peerless lustre, growing brighter as time dispels the mists which malice and prejudice have thrown about it.

The Presbyterian Church does not resent the charge of Calvinism, nor blush to have his name stand at the head of her illustrious sons. But John Calvin is not the foundation on which it is built, any more than the system of truth designated by his name rests upon his authority as its basis. His name does not occur once in the *Westminster Confession of Faith*. Not one doctrine of that historic creed is supported by any reference to his teachings. The only authorities supporting the confessional statements of the Presbyterian Church are authorities found within the lids of the Bible. Every statement is planted squarely on the infallible book. If, then, the Presbyterian Church is Calvinistic in doctrine, it is because Calvin taught the same system of truth which was taught by those who wrote 'as they were moved by the Holy Ghost'. He was a wholesale plagiarist from Moses and David, Isaiah and Ezekiel, Jesus and John, Peter and Paul.

Calvinism was the exclusive theology of the Reformation. The Protestant churches of France, Germany, Switzerland, Holland, England, and Scotland were all thoroughly Calvinistic. The great battles of the Reformation, the battles which were the birth-throes of our modern world, that secured the blessings of civil and religious liberty, were all fought and won by those whose hearts were fired, whose faith was cheered, and whose courage was nerved by the teachings of Calvin. During the most critical century of the world's history, Calvinism had the whole field to itself. There was absolutely no competing system. What of the record which it made? Was not that of all the centuries the one made most glorious by the heroic patriotism of Christian soldiers and the unconquerable fortitude of Christian martyrs? May not Calvinists look with pardonable pride on what Germany did under Luther, Switzerland under Zwingli, France under Henry of Navarre, Holland under William the Silent, England under Elizabeth, and Scotland under Knox? The mightiest influence for good that emanated from any one man during the period covered by those names emanated from John Calvin. His thought was felt by Germany and Switzerland; it was dominant among the Huguenots of France, supreme in Holland, fruitful in England, and through Knox moulded Scotland.

Nor was Calvin merely a thinker. He was as eminent for the saintliness of his life as for the splendour of his genius. Theodore Beza, his biographer, says:

> Having been an observer of Calvin's life for sixteen years, I may with perfect right testify that we have in this man a most beautiful example of a truly Christian life and death, which it is easy to calumniate, but difficult to imitate.

Professor Dorner writes:

> Calvin was equally great in intellect and character, lovely in social life, full of tender sympathy and faithfulness to friends, yielding and forgiving toward personal offences, but inexorably severe when he saw the honour of God obstinately and malignantly attacked.

If individual worth were any protection against the tongue of abuse, Calvin would need no defender. Whether Calvinism be true or false, the impartial student of history must assign Calvin a place in the very front rank of earth's greatest and best; and he must also admit that Calvinism has been one of the mightiest uplifting forces the world has known.

II. WHENCE THE NAME ARMINIANISM?

From James Arminius. He was an eminent preacher and teacher of Holland. He was born just four years before Calvin's death, and was partly educated at Geneva under Calvin's successor. When he was twenty-eight years of age he was appointed preacher at Amsterdam. While discharging the duties of this office, he was asked to refute the views of a certain layman who had attacked the doctrine of predestination. It soon developed that Arminius sympathized with the opinions of the heretical layman. A certain sermon preached about that same time tended to increase the suspicion against him. He quieted the alarm temporarily by promising to teach nothing against the *Heidelberg Catechism,* which was the recognized standard of orthodoxy in the Church of Holland. But soon another sermon brought him into fresh trouble. State and church being united, the government took notice of the alleged heresy. But before any authoritative deliverance touching his views was made he died, at the early age of forty-nine.

His teachings, however, did not die. He had sowed seed which germinated in other minds. A party crystallized around his name. The year succeeding his death his followers presented a remonstrance to the estates of Holland and Friesland. This remonstrance consisted of five articles, calling in question five of the leading doctrines of the Calvinistic theology. This gave rise to the assembling of a Synod at Dort, composed of delegates from the churches of Holland, Germany, Switzerland, and England. The first thing the Synod did was to agree that every question raised by the Arminian remonstrance should be decided by a direct appeal to the word of God. The result was the condemnation of every one of the five articles in the remonstrance, and the adoption of a number of opposite articles which were intensely Calvinistic. But this severe rebuke did not kill Arminianism. It not only lived, but grew, and the five points then in dispute have been the battleground of fierce theological strife from that day to this. They became known in subsequent history as the 'Five Points of Calvinism'. These points are:

(1) Original sin;

(2) Invincible grace;

(3) Unconditional election;

(4) Limited atonement;

(5) Perseverance of the saints.

The Arminians of Holland had rather an inglorious career. Among their number were some distinguished scholars and theologians, but they showed a tendency to growing laxity of doctrine, and soon ceased to exert any decided influence on behalf of evangelical religion. But the views of Arminius found a home in England. They were adopted and popularized by John Wesley. They were transmitted by him to his followers, and by them zealously propagated throughout Christendom. With the one exception of the church in Wales, Methodism is universally Arminian in doctrine. The other great churches of the world are committed by their confessional statements to Calvinism. It is not to be denied, however, that in some of these churches, while Calvinism is embedded in their confessions, Arminianism divides honours with it both in pulpit and pew. Lord Brougham said of one great historic church, 'it has a Romish ritual, a Calvinistic creed, and an Arminian clergy.'

For many years Calvinism and Arminianism were at deadly strife. They could not speak peaceably to one another. Experience has proven conclusively that Christ can live at peace with both. He can use both for his glory and for the saving of men. He has at length 'broken down the middle wall of partition', and abolished the enmity between them (*Eph.* 2:14-15). They exchange civilities, stand in each other's pulpits, and join hands in concerted warfare against the common enemy. This is as it should be, and it is far from our purpose to stir the embers of the old strife. We delight to sing—

> Blest be the tie that binds
> Our hearts in Christian love.

But there is no shutting our eyes to the fact that the standards of the Presbyterian Church are constructed, from foundation to turret, out of Calvinism pure and simple, the Calvinism of the Reformation period. If these standards are to mean anything to the rank and file of the church, they must be held up to view. The graciousness of their doctrines, which is somewhat obscured by the ruggedness of statement, must be exhibited. Our design in what follows is to set forth the 'Five Points', against which a considerable part of modern Christendom has revolted, in such a logical, lucid, and scriptural manner as to win for them a heartier assent from Presbyterians. We firmly believe that Calvinism was true in those dark days when at the cost of much precious blood it won its great victories for God and humanity. If true then, it is true today. If true, it should be believed and loved. 'So shall it be life unto thy soul and grace unto thy neck' (*Prov.* 3:22).

2

POINT ONE
THE FATAL IMAGE

Adam . . . begat a son in his own likeness,
after his image; and called his name Seth'
Genesis 5:3.

*L*ogically one's views of sin determine one's
views of redemption. Christ came to repair
whatever ruin was wrought by Adam. To appreci-
ate the work of the former we must understand the
work of the latter. To know just how much we are
indebted to Christ, we must know just how much we
are indebted to Adam.

Different systems of theology begin to diverge with
the doctrine of sin. Could all agree as to the disease,
they could hardly differ as to the remedy. Was Seth
born in the moral likeness of his parents? Was he a
sinner on the day of his birth? If so, was he respons-

ible for being a sinner? Was he liable to punishment for what he was by birth? Could God permit him to grow up with a sinful nature and then punish him for being a sinner? Can we blame a serpent for being vicious and venomous? The serpent is what it is by virtue of its birth from serpent parents. Is not the sinner what he is in virtue of his birth from sinful parents? 'That which is born of the flesh is flesh' (*John* 3:6) By a law as inexorable as fate, the offspring must be in essential qualities what the parents were. 'Who can bring a clean thing out of an unclean?' (*Job* 14:4).

What shall we say about Seth? What have the great thinkers of the world said about him? What do the different churches say about him in their official standards? Only three answers demand attention:

I. PELAGIUS AND PELAGIANISM

Pelagius, a preacher of the fourth century, taught that Seth inherited only the physical characteristics of Adam. He resembled his father in body, but not in soul. Pelagius taught that Adam's sin affected no one but himself, that infants are as holy in nature as

Adam was before the fall, that there can be no such thing as inherited sinfulness, or native depravity, that all sin consists in voluntary wrong-doing. In a word, Pelagius would say that a man is not reponsible for what he is, but alone for what he does. When asked why infants die if not sinful, his reply was that physical death is not the penalty of sin, that Adam would have died had he never sinned, and that infants die for the same reason that buds often fall from the stem without developing into bloom and fruit. When asked how it is that sin is universal, if all are born pure, the answer was that all are not necessarily sinners, that evil example, however, leads most astray, sooner or later. But all men, he insisted, are always able to recover themselves from sin by the power of their own wills. The only need that sinners have for the grace of God is to forgive past sins, not to restrain from sin, nor to strengthen the soul in its struggle against sin. The will is always able of itself to reject the wrong and to choose the right. Pelagius won many disciples to his views, and even to this day there are many who think as he thought. Many who never heard of Pelagius believe that every child born into the world is born pure and innocent, and that children who die go to heaven without any change of heart, or any cleansing in the blood of atonement. They believe that sin is merely a matter of wrong-doing, and that wrong-doing is always in the power of the will, so that at any time a sinner is able, without renewal of heart, to break away from sin and quit being a sinner. But Pelgianism has ever been rejected by the great majority of thoughtful and devout students of Scripture.

(a) *It fails to account for the universality of sin.* If all were born pure it is hard to believe that none should remain pure. If all tigers were born with the gentle and inoffensive dispositions of lambs, it is inconceivable that they should all become fierce and cruel. Force of example would not account for it. The only adequate explanation of the universal fierceness of tigers is that they are born with fierce propensities. In other words, the natures with which tigers are born determine them all to be fierce and cruel. Such is the only adequate explanation of the universality of sin. All are sinners, because all are born with sinful natures.

(b) *It is contradicted by consciousness.* We do not feel that all sin consists in wrong-doing. We often reproach ourselves for what we think and feel when no action results. A harsh temper is sinful; selfishness is sinful; and yet these are certainly inherited traits. The fact is that all sin lies behind the will, and therefore consists in wrong-being, and not in wrong-doing. I am culpable, not for what I do, but for what I am. This is recognized in our civil courts. Suppose I kill a man. When arraigned in court, I confess that I killed him. Does that prove me a murderer? I may have killed him accidentally. But I go further, and confess that I did it intentionally. Does this convict me of murder? I may have done it in self-defence. What is necessary in order to convict me of guilt? It is necessary to prove that I killed the man with 'malice aforethought'. The element of sin is not in the act, not in the volition of the will, but in the malice that went before and prompted the volition. In all cases the sin is in what I feel, and not in what I do.

(c) *Pelagianism is condemned by Scripture,* which clearly teaches that we are 'born in sin and conceived in iniquity' (cf. *Psa.* 51:5), and that sin is inherent in our nature. 'The carnal mind', the native disposition, 'is enmity against God, for it is not subject to the law of God, neither indeed can be' (*Rom.* 8:7). Our Saviour in his Sermon on the Mount puts all sin behind the will. Anger is murder, the impure desire is adultery. It is the bad quality in the tree that makes the fruit bad. Pelagianism is attractive at first sight, but will not bear close scrutiny.

II. JAMES ARMINIUS AND ARMINIANISM

Arminius taught that Seth was born in the moral likeness of Adam. Wesley and his followers teach the same thing. They say in their articles of religion that the 'condition of man after the fall of Adam is such that he cannot turn and prepare himself, by his own natural strength and works, to faith and calling upon God, wherefore we have no power to do good works, pleasant and acceptable to God.' According to Wesley, Adam not only ruined himself, but also his offspring, by his sin. He transmitted to Seth a nature so sinful that Seth had no power to do good works, pleasant and acceptable to God. Not only so, but when God provided salvation and suspended it on faith and prayer, Seth could not, by his own natural strength and works, turn and prepare himself to faith and calling upon God.

No one could go much beyond this in teaching the utter ruin wrought by Adam's fall. We have here the doctrine of total depravity. Man by birth is so depraved that he can do nothing acceptable to God, nor can he accept of a freely-offered salvation. He is as helpless to comply with the conditions of the gospel as to meet the demands of the law. Calvin never taught total depravity more strongly than this. But if I am born with a nature which makes it impossible for me to please God, how am I to blame for not pleasing him? If I have no power to exercise faith, how is it just to punish me for not believing? The answer which Wesleyan Arminians give to these questions is that God gives to every man sufficient grace to overcome this natural inability. The most distinctive doctrine of the Arminian system is the doctrine of 'common sufficient grace'. It is by the bestowal of this grace that God rectifies the ruin of the fall to such extent as to make man responsible, by enabling him to meet the requirements of the gospel. The operation of this grace is carefully limited. It is never sufficient to secure that any particular man shall certainly exercise faith and be saved. Such a measure of grace, Arminians think, would destroy man's freedom of will and deprive his good actions of all merit. This common grace is only sufficient to enable the will to act freely towards either good or bad, faith or unbelief, life or death.

You notice that Arminianism is brought into practical agreement with Pelagianism. Pelagianism says that man never lost the power to will that which is acceptable to God. Had he done so, he would not then have been a responsible moral agent. Arminianism says he did lose the power to will the good, and so became irresponsible, but God has restored the power and so restored the responsibility. God so far neutralized the effect of the fall, so far removed the fatal birth-heritage of Seth, as to place him once again on probation as Adam was. The test is different. To Adam God said, 'Do and live'; to Seth God said, 'Believe and live.' Such is the present position of all of Adam's posterity. They are on probation, with the lost power to will that which is acceptable to God restored to them through God's gift of common sufficient grace. What shall we say of this scheme? For one thing, it is certainly very popular. It seems an easy way to get around a serious difficulty. We are born sinners. This is too evident to admit of much question. The denial of this was the weak point in the teaching of Pelagius. Arminianism admits this. But it is hard to hold us responsible for what we cannot help: God is too gracious to do this; so he relieves us of our natal disabilities before holding us responsible.

1. *What is the real measure of this common sufficient grace?*

It makes all responsible for rejecting salvation, but does not render it certain that anyone will accept salvation. Results have made it manifest that for everyone to whom it proves a blessing, there are many to whom it proves a curse. God must have foreseen that in the case of multitudes the only result of restoring the lost ability would be the abuse of their freedom, by which they would become guilty and he would be constrained to damn them.

Take the case of Cain. God looks on him, and sees that he is born with a corrupt nature, so that if left in that condition he can never will anything acceptable to God, nor can he exercise faith in a Redeemer. God says, 'I cannot punish one who is born in that condition. He is not responsible. I will give him grace, not sufficient to certainly save him, but sufficient to enable him to exercise faith, and so enough to make him responsible. I foresee that he will abuse his restored liberty, and I shall have to damn him.' In such case would it not be gracious in God to withhold grace? If one is not responsible before grace is given, then he cannot be justly punished; and so the way for God to be most gracious is to give no grace.

It might be said that Cain, being born with a corrupt nature, must suffer even if not responsible. But how could God permit suffering to come upon one of his irresponsible creatures? Granting, however, that he might justly permit this, would it still not be more gracious in God to leave him to sufferings which were not penal than to bestow grace upon him with the certain result of punishing him afterwards with everlasting destruction? A man is in prison under sentence of death. He takes consumption. It soon becomes evident that he is going to cough himself into the grave before the day set for his execution. A doctor enters his cell and says, 'I am sorry to see you dwindling away after this fashion. Here is a remedy. It will not cure you, but it will strengthen you and keep you alive until you can be hanged.' There is not much mercy in this. But about as much as there is in common sufficient grace in all cases where it fails to save. It gives them strength of will sufficient to make them responsible and so to justify God in destroying them.

2. *Human experience furnishes no evidence that God bestows any such enabling power as is meant by common sufficient grace.*

The will is never in a state of equilibrium. It always is positively inclined for or against Christ. When it is inclined against him, the only grace that will enable it to accept him is the grace that will overcome that inclination; and when this inclination is overcome, then a positive inclination for Christ takes its place. Christ puts all wills in the one category or the other, for or against.

3. *The word of God furnishes no evidence of any common sufficient grace which God grants in order to overcome man's natural inability of will, and to render him responsible for his sins.*

It is merely a figment of the imagination, devised for the purpose of relieving a philosophical difficulty. It results from denying that man is responsible for the nature which he derives from his parents.

III. John Calvin and Calvinism

Calvin taught substantially the same view that Wesley afterwards taught as to the effect of Adam's sin on his posterity. His words are:

> We believe that all the posterity of Adam is in bondage to original sin, which is a hereditary evil. We consider that it is not necessary to inquire how sin was conveyed from one man to another; for what God had given to Adam was not for him alone, but for all his posterity; and thus in his person we have been deprived of all good things, and have fallen with him into a state of sin and misery.'

The fundamental difference between the two views is touching the responsibility of man for the corruption of nature which he inherits from Adam. We have seen that Arminianism practically agrees with Pelagianism, both denying that man is responsible for sins which result from inability of will to please God, and both denying the fact that any such inability of will now actually exists; one asserting that it never was lost, the other that it was lost by the fall, but restored by common sufficient grace.

Calvinism, on the other hand, teaches a present inability of will on the part of man, owing to his birth in sin; but that, notwithstanding this inability, he is responsible for his sinfulness, and may justly be punished of God. It says that Seth was born in the moral likeness of Adam, born a rebel against God, born in the realm and under the dominion of the devil, and that, unless he was saved by the sovereign grace of God, he grew to man's estate an enemy of God, a violator of his law, and justly merited the penalty of eternal banishment from the presence of God. Apart from the grace of God, which God might or might not grant, at his own good pleasure, a sinful career was the inevitable result of Seth's birth in sin, and yet for this inevitable result he would be responsible and justly punishable. Such is the Calvinistic view of original sin. Is it true? — not, is it palatable? A sinner's moral taste is no test.

1. *Can there be any question about a present inability to meet the requirements of God?*

'Be ye perfect, even as your Father in heaven is perfect' (*Matt.* 5:48). Such is the divine requirement. Who is able to meet it? It was the lament of Paul that he could not, even after his regeneration: 'The good that I would, I do not; but the evil which I would not, that I do' (*Rom.* 7:19). Whence this inability? From the law of sin in his members, from the corruption of nature transmitted from Adam. If this birth-heritage makes it impossible for one whom God's Spirit has regenerated to meet the divine requirements, can any measure of grace short of regeneration enable the unsaved sinner to meet those requirements? Even granting such a thing as 'common sufficient grace', we must still believe that the unrenewed man is unable to do anything acceptable to God.

2. *Can there be any question about our being blamable for this moral inability?*

Being born with corrupt natures, we can no more help being sinners than a tiger can help being a tiger. 'That which is born of the flesh is flesh' (*John* 3:6). The meaning of which is, 'that which is born sinful is sinful, and that necessarily so by the law of its nature.' The reason for the statement was to show the necessity of being born again in order to our ever seeing the kingdom of God. Yet, notwithstanding the fact that we are necessarily sinners, we reproach ourselves for being sinners. We know that we ought not to be; and when God gives his Spirit to enable us to repent, this corruption of nature, this sinful disposition which we inherit from our parents, is one of the things of which we repent. We are not only sorry for what we have done, but also for what we have been, 'hateful and hating one another' (*Titus* 3:3).

Were we not responsible for the corruption of our natures, we should not be responsible for our actual transgressions; for, as our *Confession of Faith* correctly teaches:

> From this original corruption, whereby we are utterly indisposed, disabled, and made opposite to all good, and wholly inclined to all evil, do proceed all actual transgressions.

Surely, if we are not to blame for the fountain, we are not to blame for the stream which inevitably flows from it. Moreover, our estimate of character is based upon the assumption that men are responsible for the state of their hearts. So far from our apologizing for a bad act by referring it to a bad natural disposition, we condemn it all the more severely. The bad disposition is the object of our severest reprobation. Joseph's brethren 'could not speak peaceably unto him'. Do we hold them guiltless on the ground of this inability? It merely measures the magnitude of their meanness.

3. *Do not the Scriptures lend their infallible authority to the support of this view?*

What is man's condition before regeneration? He is 'dead in trespasses and sins' (*Eph.* 2:1). If he is dead, his will must be dead, and, if so, it has never been enabled by common sufficient grace to will that which is acceptable to God. What happens to a man when he is regenerated? He is 'born again', and so becomes a 'new creature' (2 *Cor.* 5:17). If he is born again, is not his will also born again? Does it not also become new? If so, it must have been spiritually dead and helpless before. Is it not preposterous to speak of a dead sinner having a live will?

In the fifty-first Psalm David pours out his soul in penitence before God. In his confession he not only mentions actual transgressions, but also the corruption of nature from which they proceeded: 'Behold, I was shapen in iniquity, and in sin did my mother conceive me' (*Psa.* 51:5) He repented of what he was by na-ture, as well as of what he had become by practice. He did not excuse himself, nor even try to palliate his guilt by the plea that he could not help being what his birth-inheritance had made him.

If asked how it is that we are responsible for a nature that belongs to us independent of our own agency, we can only reply in the language of Romans 5:19: 'By one man's disobedience many were made sinners.' We are sinners because of Adam's sin. We may not be able to vindicate the justice of the arrangement, but so it is. We see that it is so. God's word teaches that it is so. We must accept it, and believe, if we cannot understand, that God's ways are right and his arrangements are best. All things considered, it was in keeping with the highest wisdom and goodness that Adam should act for all his posterity, and that whatever moral and spiritual condition he should secure for himself, in that moral and spiritual condition all his posterity should be born. He revolted to the standard of Satan. Under that standard all his descendants are born, and under it they prefer to live, and yet for this preference they are justly held responsible. They are not merely unfortunate, but guilty. It rests with God to save or not to save; he is under no obligation. Salvation is all of grace. 'He so loved the world as to give his only begotten Son' (*John* 3:16). It was no debt he was paying. We have no claim. Our natural inability is nothing but our natural alienation, and, instead of palliating, only aggravates, our guilt.

3

POINT TWO
AN OPENED HEART

And a certain woman named Lydia . . . heard us:
whose heart the Lord opened, that she attended
unto the things which were spoken of Paul.
Acts 16:14

*I*s God's grace in the conversion of a sinner invincible? All believe that there is a grace bestowed on sinners which they can and do resist. When God word says, 'my Spirit shall not always strive with man', it implies that men have been resisting God's Spirit. Stephen charged this very sin on the Jews, 'Ye do always resist the Holy Ghost' (Acts 7:51). The Christian consciousness confirms this teaching. We can recall times when God's Spirit moved our heart to break with sin and accept Christ, and we resisted.

But the question in dispute is, Does God in the very act of converting a sinner exercise a power which is invincible? What did God do for Lydia? Our answer to this question will depend on our views of what Lydia was able to do toward her own conversion. God did merely what Lydia could not do.

I. THE PELAGIAN VIEW

Pelagius and his followers say that Lydia was able by her own strength of will to break the fetters of sin and become a Christian. Hence, they would say that all God did for Lydia was to set before her the truth through the preaching of Paul. The apostle's instruction, logic, and persuasion did all that was necessary. Lydia did the rest.

II. THE ARMINIAN VIEW

Arminius and his followers say that Lydia's condition as a sinner was such that she could not turn and prepare herself, by her own natural strength and works, to faith and calling upon God; that she had no power to do good works, pleasant and acceptable to God, without the grace of God by Christ preventing[1] her that she might have a good will, and working with her when she had that good will. According to the Arminians, God necessarily did more than present the truth logically, eloquently, and persuasively to Lydia's mind. He bestowed prevenient and co-operating grace. He moved upon Lydia's heart before she assented to the truth, and but for this antecedent moving of God's Spirit she never would have assented.

Still the question remains, was this antecedent exercise of divine power invincible? Did God so move on Lydia's heart as to infallibly determine that she would assent to the truth? The Arminians would answer this question in the negative; for they insist that God never exercises a determining power over the sinner's heart; to do so would destroy the freedom of the will and deprive the resultant action of all moral quality. After all that God did for Lydia, she still had the determination of the matter in her own power, and might have decided it just the opposite to the way in which she actually decided it. Says Dr James Strong, in the *Schaff-Herzog Encyclopedia,*

[1] preventing: going before, preceding. *Ed.*

In a last analysis, the precise element of force which turns the scale in favour of a new life, or otherwise, is believed by the Wesleyans to be the will of the sinner himself.

Moreover, Arminians would never admit that God did anything for Lydia beyond what he did for every other woman in the congregation at the time of her conversion. The grace which enabled Lydia to accept Christ was nothing more nor less than 'common sufficient grace', it was common to all, it was sufficient for each. 'The decisive element of force which turned the scale in favour of a new life' was not the grace of God, but the will of Lydia. She, and not God, was the source of the power which made her to differ from the others. Such is the Arminian view of conversion. There would never be a conversion except for the grace of God. This grace is bestowed before the sinner exercises faith and repentance, and it stimulates and guides the energies of the soul, but it does not infallibly secure that any sinner shall ever actually exercise the faith and repentance which are necessary to salvation. Says the distinguished Arminian author, already quoted, 'without an original and continual influence from God, the will would never move in the right direction'; and yet this influence is ever subordinate to, and liable to be defeated by, the sinner's will.

III. The Calvinist View

Calvin and his followers accept the Arminian statement of Lydia's condition. It meets the requirements of both Scripture and experience to say that she could not turn and prepare herself, by her own natural strength, to faith and calling upon God; that she had no power to do good works, pleasant and acceptable to God. The divergence begins with the doctrine of 'common sufficient grace'. For what is this grace sufficient? Not to save a sinner, for many to whom it is given are lost. It is only claimed for it that it is sufficient to enable the sinner to accept Christ if he will. But the whole difficulty is in 'if he will'. He can accept Christ without any grace if he will. The invitation is, 'whosoever will, let him come' (cf. *Rev.* 22:17). It does not read, 'whosoever will, and has grace, let him come.' It does not matter about the grace, if only the sinner will.

Here is a sick man. A medicine is offered that would cure him if he would take it, but he will not take it. The doctor says, 'I am going to enable him to take it if he will.' But the only trouble is with the will. He is already able to take it if he will. It is evident that the only way to enable the sick man to take the remedy is to overcome the reluctance of his will. Is it not equally evident that the grace of God is not sufficient to enable a sinner to accept Christ unless it overcome the reluctance of his will? Whenever it does that, then it is sufficient grace, and it is just what Calvinists mean by invincible grace, it triumphs over the sinner's obstinate heart, and the result is that he accepts Christ and is saved. But common grace is not sufficient for this, otherwise all sinners would be saved.

Arminians have devised this doctrine of common sufficient grace to free man from his natural inability of will, and so to make him a responsible moral agent. Calvinists insist that no grace is needed to make him responsible. He is responsible for his inability of will, inasmuch as it is nothing else than a wicked obduracy of heart that persistently will not be subject to God. But if not responsible, then they are better off than with only such measure of grace as renders the greater part responsible only to their eternal undoing.

What did God do for Lydia? Calvinists say that he so wrought upon her heart as to secure infallibly that she would accept Christ. He did for Lydia what our catechism means by effectual calling, he convinced her of her sin and misery, enlightened her mind in the knowledge of Christ, renewed her will, and so persuaded and enabled her to embrace Jesus Christ as he is offered to us in the gospel.

Calvinists believe in enabling grace, but it is grace that actually enables.

To which of the three views does the word of God give its sanction? Let us analyze the text.

1. '*Whose heart the Lord opened.*'

What does this mean? Did the Lord open the hearts of all the other women present? Is this merely another name for 'common sufficient grace'? After God had opened Lydia's heart, was she still in a condition of unstable equilibrium, where she was liable to either accept or reject Christ? Was the question of her accepting Christ something yet to be settled by the action of her uncertain will? Have we any way by which to determine the meaning of the phrase which Luke uses to define God's agency in saving Lydia? 'Behold, I stand at the door and knock; if any man hear my voice and open the door, I will come in and sup with him and he with me' (*Rev.* 3:20). If the door is opened, that seems to settle it. Christ will certainly come in and establish a blessed fellowship. The closed door is the only barrier between the sinner and the Saviour. When, therefore, God opens the door, the barrier is taken away. Does not this language mean just what we mean by the term conversion? Did not the Lord convert Lydia? Does not to open the heart mean to change the heart, to renew the heart? How could this fundamental and vital change be more adequately described?

There is the same difference between a sinner with his heart closed and his heart opened that there is between a sinner rejecting and a sinner accepting Christ. The Lord converted Lydia. There can be no doubt of that. But he did not convert everybody else in the congregation. Hence, the grace expressed by the phrase was not common grace. God exerted a measure of power on Lydia's heart which he did not exert on the hearts of the other women. To all he may have given common grace; but to her he gave particular grace. He called all by the outward call of the gospel; he called Lydia with an effectual call, such a call as the apostle means when he says, 'Whom he called, them he also justified.'

However, there is no dispute between Calvin and Wesley touching the fact that conversion is of the Lord. John Wesley and his followers have been noted for the emphasis which they put on the supernatural character of conversion. They believe that in the case of every sinner brought from death to life the change is wrought by the direct and omnipotent power of God. What, then, is the point in dispute? This will appear as we proceed with the analysis of the text.

2. *'She attended unto the things which were spoken by Paul.'*

What does this mean? merely that she listened attentively? Was she the only attentive hearer in the congregation? Critical students of the original language tell us that 'attended unto' means that she 'gave credence unto', she believed, the things spoken by Paul. We may safely say that what Lydia did was to exercise faith in the Saviour whom Paul preached.

Now, the point in dispute is just this, did she exercise this faith before, or after, her conversion? Was it the fruit, or the antecedent condition, of her conversion? Arminius and his followers say that faith precedes and is the condition of conversion. The order is

(1) Common sufficient grace, enabling all to accept Christ, yet leaving all liable to reject him.

(2) The exercise of the sinner's will accepting Christ, which exercise of will is saving faith.

(3) The converting power of God.

> The Holy Spirit is the efficient agent which renews the moral nature of the sinner, upon the decisive act of acquiescence, as soon as it is accompanied by a positive element of acceptance, which latter is saving faith.

So writes Dr James Strong, and he claims to represent all Wesleyan Arminians. The Holy Spirit waits on the sinner to exercise saving faith before he renews his moral nature. We often hear it asserted from Arminian pulpits that God cannot save a sinner until the sinner of his own free will yields himself to God to be saved. Calvin and Calvinists say that conversion, or, to speak, more accurately, regeneration, precedes faith, that faith is the fruit of regeneration. They say that Lydia was converted before she attended unto, gave credence to, the things spoken by Paul.

3. 'That'.

This is the word which connects what God did and what Lydia did. God's work came first, then Lydia's, and the connection is expressed by the word 'that', meaning 'so that', 'to the end that'. What kind of connection is thus expressed? Causal connection. What God did was the cause of what Lydia did. His work was conversion; her work was faith; therefore conversion is the cause of faith, and not faith the cause of conversion. Is not this plain? Lydia was not converted because she exercised faith; but she exercised faith because she was converted.

We return now to the question with which we began, was not the grace which saved Lydia invincible grace? Did it not triumph over all opposition? Was it not invincible for the reason that it did not wait on the decision of Lydia's will, but taking the initiative, overcame the resistance of her will? She was not constrained against her will; but when God opened her heart, then the very thing which she wanted to do was to accept Christ. It would have done violence to the law of her new life to have rejected him.

Was her case exceptional? Manifestly not.

(a) *Invincible grace in conversion is the logical corollary of the sinner's 'death in trespasses and sin'.*

No grace can avail to save a dead sinner but such as quickens into life; and the grace that does this leaves no place for resistance. The quickened sinner is already saved. Those were saved to whom Paul wrote, 'And you did he quicken, when ye were dead through your trespasses and sins' (*Eph.* 2:1).

(b) *Invincible grace is implied in the language used to describe conversion:*

'I will take away the stony heart out of your flesh, and give you an heart of flesh' (*Ezek.* 36:26). Instead of waiting on the will to act, he so changes the nature that lies behind the will as to secure infallibly that the will will not oppose his grace.

(c) *The Scriptures assert expressly that God's grace controls the will.*

'God . . . worketh in you both to will and to do of his good pleasure' (*Phil.* 2:13). God secured obedience to his will by working in us to the extent of controlling our wills. 'Thy people shall be willing in the day of thy power' (*Psa.* 110:3). His power is not constraining, but renewing; it gives a new heart, and so secures new willing. There are some who believe that God can powerfully touch every part of man's nature except his will, but that God has given to the will an autocracy that makes it independent of its Maker. But the will is not a sovereign, merely a subject; not a master, merely a menial. What the heart commands the will executes. He, therefore, who can change the heart can never have any trouble about controlling the will.

(d) *Practically, all evangelical Christians believe in the invincibility of divine grace.*

We show this faith in our prayers. Some years ago I heard an Arminian preacher close a very earnest and impressive sermon to the unconverted with this statement: 'Now, sinners, I have done all that I can do, and God has done all that he can do, and so your salvation rests with you.' He then called on me to pray. It occurred to me that it must be a waste of breath to pray to a God who had already exhausted his resources. If the whole matter rested with the sinner, then he was the proper person to plead with in prayer. But the preacher had been pleading with the sinner for the last hour most earnestly and ably. It seemed rather an embarrassing position. What did I do? Just what the preacher wished me to do, and expected me to do; just what he would have done had he led the prayer: I asked God to do more than he had done; asked him to come in 'convicting and converting power'; asked him to bestow invincible grace.

When on their knees, the Arminians and Calvinists agree in ascribing to God absolute power over his creatures, and in entreating him to do what he could not do if man's will were independent of his control. All Christians blend their grateful voices in singing:

> Grace led my roving feet
>   To tread the heavenly road,
> And new supplies each hour I meet,
>   While pressing on to God.
>
> Grace taught my soul to pray,
>   And made mine eyes o'erflow;
> 'T'was grace that kept me to this day,
>   And will not let me go.

4

POINT THREE
FIRST CHOICE

Ye have not chosen me, but I have chosen you.
John 15:16

Who makes the first choice, Christ or the sinner? Your answer to this question decides whether you are Calvinist or Arminian. If you say that Christ chooses the sinner, and in consequence of this the sinner chooses Christ, you are a Calvinist. If you say that a sinner chooses Christ, and in virtue of this Christ chooses the sinner, you are an Arminian.

Both Calvinist and Arminian believe in election. It is a doctrine standing out conspicuously on the surface of both Old and New Testaments. The Jews were an elect nation before Christ. 'For thou art an holy people unto the Lord thy God; the Lord hath chosen thee to be a peculiar people unto himself, above all peoples that are upon the earth' (*Deut.* 14:2). God selected the Jews from among the nations, gave them special revelations of his love, exercised over them a peculiarly gracious providence, and made them parties to covenants in which his mercy was signally displayed. 'He sheweth his word unto Jacob, his statutes and judgments unto Israel. He hath not dealt so with any nation: and as for his judgments, they have not known them' (*Psa.* 147:19-20). Not only did God choose Israel as a nation, but out of this elect nation he chose individuals. 'I will bring forth a seed out of Jacob, and out of Judah an inheritor of my mountains; and mine elect shall inherit it, and my servants shall dwell there' (*Isa.* 65:9).

On the pages of the New Testament the fact of an election still confronts us. 'For the elect's sake, whom he hath chosen, he hath shortened the days' (*Mark* 13:20). 'Shall not God avenge his own elect?' asks our Saviour (*Luke* 18:7). And Paul shouts out the challenge, 'Who shall lay any thing to the charge of God's elect?' (*Rom.* 8:33). It is too manifest to admit of question, that during all the centuries covered by the history of God's inspired book he had a people whom he had chosen from the rest of mankind, and whom he designated as his elect.

What shall we say about this election? What have the great thinkers of the world said about it? What have the great churches of the world said about it in their official formularies? Going back to the Reformation, look at the statements of the historic churches:

The Swiss: 'God has, from the beginning, freely and of his mere grace, without any respect of men, predestinated or elected the saints, whom he will save in Jesus Christ.'

The Waldenses: 'God saves from this corruption and condemnation those whom he has chosen from the foundation of the world, not for any foreseen disposition, faith or holiness in them, but of his mercy in Jesus Christ his Son.'

Dutch: 'God delivers and preserves from perdition all whom he in his eternal and unchangeable counsel of mere goodness hath elected in Christ Jesus our Lord, without any respect to their works.'

Scots: 'That same eternal God and Father, who of mere grace elected us in Christ Jesus his Son, before the foundation of the world was laid, appointed him to be our head, our brother, our pastor, and great bishop of our souls.'

English: 'Predestination to life is the everlasting purpose of God, whereby, before the foundations of the world were laid, he hath constantly decreed by his counsel, secret to us, to deliver from curse and damnation those whom he hath chosen in Christ out of mankind, and to bring them by Christ to everlasting salvation as vessels made to honour.'

French: 'From this corruption and general condemnation in which all men are plunged, God, according to his eternal and immutable counsel, calleth those whom he hath chosen by his goodness and mercy alone in our Lord Jesus Christ, without consideration of their works, to display in them the riches of his mercy.'

From this review it appears that Protestant Christendom was united in its belief touching election in those days when men had to contend for their faith even unto death. It is doubtful whether at any other period men have thought more carefully or more profoundly on the teachings of God's word. When a man had to stake his all upon the creed which he professed, he was not likely to commit himself to it thoughtlessly. During all that heroic period when the blood of the martyrs was buying for us the blessings of civil and religious liberty, there was perfect agreement in all the churches that were standing against Rome in professing the belief that God has from eternity, of his mere good pleasure, without reference to any foreseen faith and good works in man, chosen a people for himself to be redeemed by Christ, called and sanctified by his Spirit.

In our own day there are two views dividing evangelical Christendom, the Arminian and the Calvinistic.

I. THE ARMINIAN VIEW OF ELECTION

The Arminian view is that election has a twofold meaning in Scripture:

1. *It means the choice of certain nations to the possession of religious privileges.*

The Jews were chosen to enjoy the advantage of an inspired revelation of truth, and the external benefits of church organization. Today God is shedding gospel light on some nations, while others are left in darkness. Such an election confers great benefits of a temporal and external kind, but not the blessing of salvation.

2. It also means the choice of certain individuals to eternal life on foresight of their faith and repentance, and perseverance in evangelical obedience.

God's election is concerned primarily with character, and individuals put themselves in the category of the elect by acquiring the character which God demands.

Probably the generality of Arminians would concur in the statement of Bishop Whately,

> we may conclude that no Christian is elected to eternal life absolutely, but only to the knowledge of the gospel, to the privileges of the Christian church, to the offer of God's Holy Spirit, and to the promise of final salvation on condition of being a faithful follower of Christ.

The Arminian view of election follows consistently from the Arminian view of conversion. If, 'in the last analysis, the decisive influence which turns the scale in favour of the new life is the sinner's own will', then, of course, God's choice of the sinner must wait on that last decisive act of the sinner's will. God's choice is conditioned on the sinner's choice, and is from eternity only because God foreknows from eternity what the sinner's choice will be.

II. THE CALVINISTIC VIEW OF ELECTION

The Calvinistic view is the one contained in all the creeds of the Reformation churches. It includes especially these three points:

1. It means the choice of individuals.

2. It has for its end their eternal salvation.

3. It is not conditioned on the foresight of their character.

1. *It means the choice of individuals.*

Nothing is said to the contrary when it is asserted that God elects nations. Individuals constitute nations, and nations are made up exclusively of individuals. God chose the Jewish nation. This means that he chose the individuals, Abraham, Isaac, and Jacob, and their individual descendants. Whenever God discriminates between nations, he is discriminating between individuals. Take the knotty text, Romans 9:11-12:

> For the children being not yet born, neither having done any good or evil, that the purpose of God according to election might stand, not of works, but of him that calleth; it was said unto her, The elder shall serve the younger.

Arminians will not allow that God discriminated in this apparently arbitrary manner between the two individuals, Esau and Jacob. They say that these names stand for two nations, the Edomites and the Jews. Does this interpretation alter the principle involved? Were not the Edomites individuals as really as Esau was an individual? Were not the Jews individuals in the same sense in which Jacob was an individual? Why should it be allowable in God to discriminate between fathers and their families, and not between fathers irrespective of their families? If there is impropriety at all, is it not all the greater when the discrimination extends to the unborn descendants? Might not Esau expostulate, with some show of reason, 'O God, if thou must needs put a difference between Jacob and me, giving him the dominion over me, surely thou canst not justly include my innocent children in the judgment?' Is anything gained in the way of avoiding difficulty by supposing that God's election has to do with nations? Does not such an election rather increase the difficulty, for the reason that it must necessarily leave out all consideration of individual merit, and thereby become liable in an eminent degree to the charge of arbitrariness?

But, as a matter of fact, the object of God's choice is not nations but individuals. The design of Paul in his reference to election was to show that God never dealt with Israel in a lump. He separated between Abraham's children, choosing Isaac and rejecting Ishmael. He separated between Rebecca's children, choosing Jacob and rejecting Esau; thus demonstrating that he had ever acted according to his sovereign pleasure, regardless of racial lines, discriminating not only between Jew and Gentile, but also between Jew and Jew.

Notice the use which Paul makes of this fact in answering the perplexing question, 'hath God cast away his people?' (*Rom.* 11:1). It would seem so, if the Jews, as a nation, were his people, for the kingdom was rapidly passing from them to the Gentiles. Paul's answer is, 'God hath not cast away his people which he foreknew' (*Rom.* 11:2). His elect people were not the Jews as a nation. The two were never synonymous. In the days of Elijah, out of the whole nation God had only seven thousand elect ones. Referring to this, the apostle adds, 'Even so then at this present time also there is a remnant according to the election of grace' (*Rom.* 11:5). God's elect, as defined by Paul in the eighth chapter of Romans, are all those who love God and who are called according to his purpose.

2. Election is to eternal life.

Those who insist on nations, and not individuals, as the object, connect with this view the idea that election is only to certain religious privileges.

Take again the knotty text, Romans 9:11-12 — Arminians not only hold that these names stand for nations, but further, that the favour shown to Jacob and his posterity was merely to the extent of giving them the knowledge of the true God, and blessing them with the external advantages of a true worship. 'He sheweth his word unto Jacob; his statutes and judgments unto Israel.' Arminians recognize the fact that these blessings were of great value. They made this present life worth more; they made eternal life a possibility to every child of Jacob; and they actually resulted in the eternal salvation of a multitude of Jacob's posterity.

We may well inquire what is the difference in principle between God's electing the Jews to this measure of blessing and his electing certain individuals to the larger blessing of eternal life? If God may lift a whole nation to a high vantage ground, open to them the door of deliverance, bless them with such knowledge and ply them with such motives as will certainly result in the salvation of many among them, while he leaves another nation, descended from the same parents, down in the depths with the unrelieved shadow of sin resting on them, 'without God and without hope in the world', why may he not, with equal propriety, crown one sinner with the blessing of an endless life, while he leaves another to die under the righteous sentence of his law? The difference in the measure of grace bestowed makes no difference in the principle involved.

But, as a matter of fact, election does not mean merely the choosing of certain persons, or nations, to the enjoyment of religious privileges. Paul marks a difference between the Jewish nation to whom the external advantages of religion belonged, and the 'remnant according to the election of grace'. God's elect are defined as those who have been predestinated to be conformed to the image of God's Son; they are those who are so joined to Christ that nothing can ever separate them from his love. They are put by our Saviour in sharp contrast with those who merely enjoy the outward advantages of the gospel, 'many are called', i.e., have all the opportunities that the gospel can give, 'but few are chosen' (*Matt.* 22:14).

Election is something entirely different from external religious advantages. It is something which frees the soul from all the disasters and perils into which sin had brought it. It is in a tone of victorious defiance that Paul asks, 'Who shall lay anything to the charge of God's elect?' They are out of danger, because God is unchangeably on their side. 'We are bound to give thanks alway to God for you . . . because [he] hath from the beginning chosen you to salvation' (2 *Thess.* 2:13). The motive of Paul's thanksgiving was not that God had conferred upon them religious advantages, but that God had chosen them to salvation, elected them to eternal life.

3. *Election is not conditioned on any foresight of the sinner's character or conduct.*

This is the main point in dispute. According to Wesley and his followers, God gives 'common sufficient grace' to all, and then leaves the destiny of each sinner to the decision of his free, uncontrollable will. If the sinner, without further agency on God's part, makes a movement toward God, then, and not till then, God bestows the blessings of pardon and salvation. The reason why John was saved and Judas was not saved was that John made a better use of common grace. God did no more for John than for Judas until John, in the use of grace common to both, exercised faith in the Lord Jesus Christ. On the foresight of this faith God elected John to salvation.

What does Christ mean when he says, 'Ye have not chosen me, but I have chosen you'? (*John* 15:16). Does he not make this statement by way of explaining the vital union between him and his disciples? This saving relationship had its origin in his choice, not in theirs. The only other interpretation of Christ's statement is to suppose that he was referring to his choice of the twelve to official position. But is it not altogether improbable that he would interject a statement with such a limited application in the midst of a discourse which in all its other parts certainly deals with truths applicable to all disciples? We cannot restrict the teaching of the context to the apostles. 'I am the vine, ye are the branches' (*John* 15:5). Who are the 'ye'? Evidently all disciples.

Equally evident is it that throughout the chapter the instruction comprehends the relations, privileges, and duties of all disciples. Judas was absent, and all that was spoken to the eleven was spoken to them as the representatives of all believers. Christ chooses first in all cases. 'We love him because he first loved us' (*1 John* 4:19), and likewise we choose him because he first chooses us. This is made further evident by such considerations as the following:

(1) *Faith and penitence, the initial graces of the Christian life, are the gifts of God.*

Speaking of Christ, Peter says, 'Him hath God exalted a Prince and a Saviour, for to give repentance . . . and remission of sins' (*Acts* 5:31). The sinner never repents until moved thereto by Christ. The writer to the Hebrews calls Jesus 'the author and finisher of our faith' (*Heb.* 12:2). The sinner never exercises faith until the power to do so is conferred by Christ. But faith and repentance are the beginning of salvation. If, then, these are from Christ, the beginning is from him, not from the sinner. 'By grace are ye saved through faith; and that not of yourselves, it is the gift of God' (*Eph.* 2:8). The Gentiles in Antioch of Pisidia received the word of the Lord gladly, 'and as many as were ordained to eternal life believed.' Their election to eternal life preceded and was the cause of their faith. The Lord opened Lydia's heart, and then she believed the things spoken by Paul. In every case the divine agency is first, and the sinner's agency follows as the consequence.

(2) *The very object of election is to secure these virtuous exercises of the soul, and, therefore, they cannot be the ground or condition of election.*

In Ephesians 1:4 the apostle declares that God 'hath chosen us in [Christ] before the foundation of the world, that we should be holy and without blame before him in love.' Why were we chosen? Not because of our faith and repentance, not because we were holy, but in order that we should be holy. God chooses us in our sins that he may make us holy. 'Whom he did foreknow, he also did predestinate to be conformed to the image of his Son' (*Rom.* 8:29). The very object of the predestination is to bring about conformity to Christ.

There is scarcely a hint in the Bible that election is based on God's foresight of faith and repentance. It is a theory of human invention to get around supposed difficulties. Hence, we mention as a strong confirmation of the Calvinistic view,

(3) *Paul's method of dealing with the difficulties of election.*

He cited the case of God's discriminating in favour of Rebecca's younger son as an instance of unconditional election, laying stress on the fact that the discrimination was made before the children were born, or had done any good or evil. At once a difficulty emerges. 'What shall we say then? Is there unrighteousness with God?' (*Rom.* 9:14). 'Indeed there is', says the Arminian, 'if you mean precisely what you say; for it would be unrighteous in God to make a difference between two individuals, except on the ground that one is better, or more obedient, or more yielding, or more something than the other. God must treat all alike until men make themselves to differ.'

How does Paul deal with the difficulty? He simply affirms that such a discrimination is not unrighteous: 'For he saith to Moses, I will have mercy on whom I will have mercy, and I will have compassion on whom I will have compassion. So then it is not of him that willeth, nor of him that runneth, but of God that showeth mercy' (*Rom.* 9:15-16). The argument is that it cannot be unrighteous in God to put a difference between men without respect to their willing, or running, for it is the very prerogative which he asserts his right to exercise. The fact that God claims such prerogative proves there is nothing unrighteous in the exercise of it. 'Thou wilt say then . . . why doth he yet find fault? For who hath resisted his will?' (*Rom.* 9:19). 'Indeed, I will say just that very thing', says the Arminian. 'If God decides the destinies of men in this sovereign, arbitrary manner, the sinner is not responsible. If he is to be saved, he will be saved; if he is to be lost, he will be lost. The whole business is already settled. He may as well fold his hands and wait the inevitable.'

How does Paul deal with this difficulty? He first rebukes the irreverence of such a cavil: 'Nay but, O man, who art thou that repliest against God? Shall the thing formed say to him that formed it, Why hast thou made me thus?' (*Rom.* 9:20). Then, instead of modifying or softening down his assertion of divine sovereignty, and so relieving the difficulty, he gives it a balder and more offensive statement: 'Hath not the potter power over the clay, of the same lump to make one vessel unto honour, and another unto dishonour?' (*Rom.* 9:21).

If Paul had been teaching the Arminian view of election, it is inconceivable that he should have provoked such objections. But if by any possibility he had provoked such objections, it is inconceivable that he should have dealt with them after such manner. The objections with which he deals are the common and the most formidable objections to the Calvinistic view of election; and instead of obviating them by explaining away the Calvinism of his teaching, he simply rebukes them as an impertinence and deepens the blue of his Calvinism.

(4) *The Calvinistic view is in perfect agreement with the teachings of Scripture touching original sin and the new birth.*

The problem is to save a spiritually dead sinner. God solves the problem by imparting spiritual life. When Jesus, standing by the grave, cried with a loud voice, 'Lazarus, come forth' (*John* 11:43), did Lazarus respond to the command before Christ imparted life? Was the life the result of his obedience to Christ, or was his obedience to Christ the result of life? Could there be any, even the slightest, response, until life was imparted? If, then, the sinner's condition is one of spiritual death, can he respond to God's offer of mercy, even to the extent of faith and penitence until he is born again, until he is quickened into life by the Spirit of God? If not, then God's choice must precede his. Mr Spurgeon says,

The Romanists have an extraordinary miracle of their own about St Dennis, of whom they tell the lying legend, that after his head was off he took it up in his hands and walked with it two thousand miles; whereupon said a wit, 'so far as the two thousand miles go, it is nothing at all, it is only the first step in which there is any difficulty.'

So we believe about salvation. If the dead sinner could take the first step that is involved in faith and repentance, without having first felt the life-giving touch of God's power, we see no reason why he could not take all the other steps involved in his salvation.

(5) *All prayer for the conversion of sinners is based on the Calvinistic view of election.*

Arminians teach that God, in giving common sufficient grace, has done enough for the sinner, and that he will do nothing more until the sinner does something.

Why, then, do they pray for the conversion of sinners? Evidently they believe that God can do more, and they ask and expect him to do more. They ask God to send his Holy Spirit and work conviction in the hearts of sinners; they ask God to add special grace to common grace.

Moreover, they pray to God to exercise discriminating mercy, for they ask him to do for certain sinners to whom they are preaching the gospel what he has not done and is not doing for sinners all over the world. Suppose God answers their prayer, and by a special outpouring of his Spirit saves the sinners for whom they are interceding, is not this election? What more claim have these sinners on God than those in China? Yet, in answer to the prayers of his servants, he bestows on them the blessing of eternal life. He chooses them before they choose him. Here is election, based not on foresight of the sinner's faith and penitence, but on foresight of prayer in his behalf.

Calvinism is the only creed that will bear translation into prayer.

Whoever truly prays ascribes nothing to his own will or power except the sin that condemns him before God, and knows of nothing that could endure the judgment of God except it be wrought within him by the divine love. But while all other tendencies in the church preserve this attitude so long as their prayer lasts, to lose themselves in radically different conceptions as soon as the amen has been pronounced, the Calvinist adheres to the truth of his prayer in his confession, in his theology, in his life; and the amen that has closed his petition re-echoes in the depth of his consciousness and throughout the whole of his existence.

Ever the Calvinist, if true to his faith, has his heart tuned to the doxology: 'Not unto us, O Lord, not unto us, but unto thy name give glory, for thy mercy, and for thy truth's sake' (*Psa.* 115:1).

> 'Tis not for works which we have done,
>   Or shall hereafter do,
> But He of His abounding love
>   Salvation does bestow.
>
> The glory, Lord, from first to last,
>   Is due to Thee alone;
> Aught to ourselves we dare not take,
>   Or rob Thee of Thy crown.

5

POINT FOUR
BOUNDARY LINES

For therefore we both labour and suffer reproach,
because we trust in the living God, who is the Saviour
of all men, specially of those that believe.
1 Timothy 4:10

*I*s the atonement limited in its design and scope? When God gave his only begotten Son as an expression of his love for the world, did he design by this costly gift to provide salvation for the whole race of mankind? Was the gift an expression of indiscriminating love? Was it meant for one sinner as really and fully as for another?

I. The Arminian View of the Atonement

Arminius and his followers declare that

> Jesus Christ, the Saviour of the world, died for all men and for every man, so that he has obtained for them all, by his death on the cross, redemption and the forgiveness of sins; yet no one actually enjoys this forgiveness of sins except the believer.

Wesley states the matter thus:

> The offering of Christ, once made, is that perfect redemption, propitiation, and satisfaction for all the sins of the whole world, both original and actual.

These statements seem to mean that Jesus Christ, by his death, paid the penalty of every man's sins, and so procured for every man the blessings of redemption and forgiveness. But if this were the meaning of the authors, then the logical result would be universal salvation. If Christ has actually paid the penalty of my sins, it would not be right in God to make me pay it again. A just judge cannot exact payment for the same debt twice. Dr Whitby, a recognized authority among the Arminians, thus defines their doctrine:

When we say that Christ died for all, we do not mean that he hath purchased actual pardon, or reconciliation, or life for all; this being in effect to say that he procured an actual remission of sins to unbelievers, and actually reconciled God to the impenitent and disobedient, which is impossible. He only by his death hath put all men in a capacity of being justified and pardoned, and so of being reconciled to and having peace with God upon their turning to God and having faith in our Lord Jesus Christ; the death of Christ having rendered it consistent with the justice and wisdom of God, with the honour of his majesty and with the ends of government to pardon the penitent believer.

The doctrine, as thus explained, is very far removed from universalism. The death of Christ does not purchase for any sinner actual pardon or remission of sin. It has no specific relation to any individual sinner. It is a universal remedy for the sinful condition of the race, intended equally for the benefit of all, but made available only on conditions which each sinner is left to fulfil or not in the exercise of his self-determining will. The death of Christ puts all in a salvable condition, but renders the salvation of no one certain. It merely removes all legal obstacles out of God's way, so that without offence to his majesty or hurt to his government he can pardon and receive the penitent sinner. So far as the purpose of God is concerned, the remedy is as truly for those who persistently reject it as for those who penitently accept it.

This view of the atonement is logically a companion doctrine of common sufficient grace. Arminianism abhors the idea of God's making discriminations between sinners who are equally guilty and equally needy. The atonement is for each and all alike, making the salvation of all possible, leaving the salvation of each dependent on the exercise of his own will. Common sufficient grace is for each and all alike, making it possible for all to accept the common remedy, leaving it possible for each to reject it. God provides a universal remedy, gives universal grace, and leaves results with man. So far as God's agency is concerned, all may be saved, or all may be lost.

It is not to be denied that there is much plausibility in this view. It seems altogether reasonable that God should treat all the children of Adam alike; that if he provides an atonement for one, he will provide it for all. 'He is good to all, and his tender mercies are over all his works' (*Psa.* 145:9).

Moreover, it costs him no more to make provision for all than for a part. Nothing less than the gift of his only begotten Son will avail to save a part; the same gift is of sufficient value to save all. To limit the beneficent design of an atonement, already provided, and fully adequate to the needs of the whole race, would seem gratuitous unkindness.

Above all, the word of God, in many texts, seems to teach this most reasonable view of the atonement. 'Behold the Lamb of God which taketh away the sin of the world' (*John* 1:29). How universal the scope of the great sacrifice! 'God so loved the world, that he gave his only begotten Son, that whosoever believeth in him should not perish' (*John* 3:16). How impartial this world-embracing love! 'He is the propitiation for our sins, and not for our's only but also for the sins of the whole world' (*1 John* 2:2). Jesus was 'made a little lower than the angels . . . that he by the grace of God should taste death for every man' (*Heb.* 2:9). What could be more clear and emphatic? Then in perfect harmony with these Scriptures are the broad and generous invitations of the gospel: 'If any man thirst, let him come unto me and drink' (*John* 7:37). 'Whosoever will, let him take the water of life freely' (*Rev.* 22:17). Does not a universal invitation mean a universal remedy? The great commission reads, 'Go ye into all the world and preach the gospel to every creature' (*Mark* 16:15). Where is the sincerity and the integrity of Christ, if he bids us offer the benefits of his death unto every man, unless those benefits were designed for every man?

By such a course of argument do our Arminian brethren make their view appear both pleasing and plausible, and at the same time they make the contrary view appear odious and dishonouring to God. Let us suspend judgment, however, until we take a careful look at the other side.

II. THE CALVINISTIC VIEW OF THE ATONEMENT

Calvinists have ever held that the atonement has a direct and personal reference to God's elect people. While they do not deny that Christ died in some sense for all men, yet they believe that his death was specifically a vicarious punishment for the sins of those, and only those, who are actually justified and saved.

An underlying difference between Arminianism and Calvinism is, that according to the former, God's agency in saving sinners is general and indefinite; while according to the latter, his agency is always specific and personal. As the doctrine of an indefinite atonement matches the doctrine of common sufficient grace, so the doctrine of a limited specific atonement matches the doctrine of special, efficacious grace. Hence, in Calvinistic creeds, the doctrine of the atonement is set forth in connection with the doctrine of election. We see this in the answer to the twentieth question in our *Shorter Catechism:*

> God, having, out of his mere good pleasure, from all eternity, elected some to everlasting life, did enter into a covenant of grace, to deliver them out of the estate of sin and misery, and to bring them into an estate of salvation, by a Redeemer.

Note the order of thought in the divine purpose. God selects from the mass of fallen humanity a people for himself; he enters into a covenant with Christ in their behalf; by virtue of this covenant Christ becomes their Redeemer. According to this view, the atonement is a means for accomplishing God's purpose in election. It has specific reference therefore to the elect, and whatever benefits it confers on others are incidental and subordinate to its main design. In the *Confession of Faith,* Chapter VIII, Article 5, it is declared that

> the Lord Jesus, by his perfect obedience and sacrifice of himself, which he through the eternal Spirit once offered up unto God, hath fully satisfied the justice of his Father, and purchased not only reconciliation, but

an everlasting inheritance in the kingdom of heaven,
for all those whom the Father hath given unto him.

One characteristic of this view, which is characteristic of the whole Calvinistic system, is that it represents God as having a clear-cut plan before his mind, and as selecting means with reference to the certain, infallible execution of that plan. He purposes nothing beyond what he fully determines to accomplish. He intends nothing over and above that which he executes. Instead of providing a general atonement which merely makes salvation possible to all, but certain to none, he provides an atonement for the definite purpose of saving those whom he had previously determined to save.

We can make the exact point in dispute between Arminians and Calvinists stand out in more clear-cut outline by noting the several points of agreement. They agree:

(1) That the atonement is sufficient for all.

(2) That it is exactly adapted to the needs of all.

(3) That it will certainly avail for all, if they will only accept it.

(4) That it is freely and sincerely offered to all.

(5) That it confers many temporal benefits on all.

(6) That, as a matter of fact, its saving benefits are limited to those who believe.

So far all are agreed. 'The atonement is sufficient for all, efficient only for believers.' The point at issue is, Did God intend the efficiency to be co-extensive with the sufficiency? or did God intend that while the atonement should be unlimited in its sufficiency, it should be limited in its efficiency? Did he design to save all by it? or did he design to save only those who are actually saved by it? Does the result, which is the salvation of only a part of the race, reveal God's design? or does this result reveal the failure of God's design? Did Christ die, in the same sense, for everybody? for Moses and Pharaoh? for Ruth and Jezebel? for John and Judas? for James and Herod? for Paul and Nero? for the martyr and his executioner? The Arminian says, 'Yes, the atonement, in the intent and purpose of God, was for all alike.' The Calvinist says, 'No, the atonement was designed of God to secure just the results which have been accomplished by it—many temporal blessings for all the world, but the blessing of eternal life for only a part of the world.'

Which of these views is true? We have seen that the views of our Arminian friends can be made to appear exceedingly plausible; and what is more, they seem to be supported by a good array of Scripture. It sounds well, and seems reasonable, that God should include all sinners in the provisions of his grace, and place them all on an equal footing. But we want the truth. It may turn out that 'God's ways are not our ways, nor his thoughts our thoughts.' We should have thought in advance that God would not suffer his sinless child Adam to be tempted by the devil, knowing that the result would be an endless development of ever-increasing sin and sorrow. We are not competent to say in advance that God will make no discrimination between sinners equally guilty and, equally needy. We are competent to say after the result that he has discriminated. All children are not born into the world equally favoured by God's providence. At the time of writing there are some twenty millions of cannibals in Africa. Do the children born of those savage tribes, whose language contains no word for God, whose minds have never been penetrated by one single ray of gospel light, stand an equally fair chance of being saved with the children of Christian parents in England and America? If so, all zeal for foreign missions is nonsense. All children, even in Christian lands, are not equally favoured in the circumstances of their birth and training. If, then, this world is under the government of a divine providence, that providence discriminates between sinners, and that before they have 'done any good or evil' (*Rom.* 9:11). Once grant that God discriminates, and we cannot reason on general principles about the atonement. If his providence decides that a child born of savage parents shall grow up in the wilds of Africa without ever hearing of the atonement, it is hard to conceive that God designed or intended the atonement for that child. There are other considerations which lead us to question whether the death of Christ had an indiscriminate reference to the salvation of all men.

1. Did he die to atone for the sins of the multitude of sinners whose fate was long since sealed before his advent into the world? Did he die to save those who perished in the flood, and in the plains of Sodom?

2. Did he die to save those to whom he does not give the graces of faith and repentance?

3. Did he die to atone for those for whom he does not intercede? 'I pray not for the world, but for them which thou hast given me out of the world' (*John* 17:9).

4. Did Christ die with the expectation of saving any others than those whom he actually does save? 'My sheep hear my voice, and I know them, and they follow me: and I give unto them eternal life' (*John* 10:27-28). Christ's purpose could not have been larger than his expectation, therefore he did not purpose to save all, and did not die to atone for all.

Calvinists believe that the atonement has both a general and a specific reference. It is general in its design:

(a) in that it displays the compassion of God toward all, for he would save them if they would accept;

(b) in that it demonstrates the obduracy of sinners in rejecting so great a mercy, for it is their fault that they do not accept Christ; and,

(c) in that it secures for all the manifold blessings which they enjoy in this life.

It is limited in design, in that it secures actual pardon and salvation for only a part of the sinful human race. He is 'the Saviour of all men, specially of those that believe' (*1 Tim.* 4:10). He is the Saviour of all men in a lower sense, in a smaller degree, than of those who believe. He secures for all a postponement of the doom incurred by their sins; he secures for believers eternal exemption from the doom. This is just what he intended to do by his death. 'I . . . know my sheep . . . and I lay down my life for my sheep' (*John* 10:14-15).

After all, it is largely a difference touching words and names. Arminians believe that the atonement is limited in its application to those who believe; Calvinists believe nothing more and nothing less. Inasmuch, however, as Calvinists believe that God makes the application, they say that the atonement is limited in design as well as in application. But there is nothing in their view to prevent their offering Christ to every sinner, and assuring him, on the authority of God, that, if he will accept, he shall be saved. 'Ho, every one that thirsteth, come ye to the waters' (*Isa* 55:1).

This is good Calvinism; and if anyone holds to a Calvinism that does not square with the widest offers of God's mercy, then he has gotten hold of a spurious article, and the sooner he flings it away the better. 'Whosoever will, let him take the water of life freely' (*Rev.* 22:17). Any so-called Calvinism that does not chime with this sweet gospel bell deserves to 'be cast out, and to be trodden under foot of men' (*Matt.* 5:13). We ask for no leniency of judgment on any argument or inference that would tend to make the strait gate straiter, or the narrow way more narrow. Above all things, let us believe that 'Christ Jesus came into the world to save sinners' (*1 Tim.* 1:15), and that 'him that cometh to him he will in no wise cast out' (cf. *John* 6:37).

6

POINT FIVE
GRACE LINKED TO GLORY

*Being confident of this very thing, that he which
hath begun a good work in you will perform it until
the day of Jesus Christ.*
Philippians 1:6

*I*s it true that 'once in grace always in grace'? Is it
true that the beginning and the end of our salvation are so linked together that they never are, and
never can be, severed? In other words, when does a
penitent sinner, seeking salvation, pass the crisis of
his eternal destiny? Is it the moment when he is born
again and accepts Christ as his Saviour? or is it some
moment beyond death when he passes the gates of
pearl and enters the celestial city?

This is an exceedingly interesting inquiry, and one of no ordinary magnitude. If I am a Christian, am I now eternally safe? or does my final condition remain a matter of uncertainty until the day of my departure from earth? Arminians and Calvinists are on opposite sides of this question. The former hold that a true Christian, who today is a child of God, in the full enjoyment of his favour, may tomorrow be an outcast from God, a child of the devil, and under the sentence of death. The latter hold that a child of God, in the full enjoyment of his favour today, is as safe as he will be when the issues of the judgment are announced and he takes possession of his heavenly mansion.

I. THE ARMINIAN VIEW OF PERSEVERANCE

The Arminian view is thus stated by Dr James Strong:

Holding to the view that the human will has the fearful power to accept or reject salvation, Wesleyans, without exception, believe that this power equally extends to the retention or loss of the divine pardon, peace and purity at any period during probation. They, therefore, reject the doctrine of the impossibility of lapsing utterly and finally from grace, and believe that any may, and many do, lose their state of acceptance, and their love of holy things, and ultimately perish.

Dr Strong suggests what is manifestly true, that the doctrine of 'falling from grace' results logically from the Arminian doctrine of the will. If the will of man is free in such sense that God cannot determine it certainly to the choice of salvation, then it must follow that God cannot determine it certainly to the continued preference of salvation. If God cannot control the will of the sinner to the acceptance of Christ, he cannot control the will of the Christian to the retention of Christ.

A fundamental postulate of Arminianism is that the human will, as a distinct faculty of the soul, is always free from control. No matter what the dispositions which lie back of it, no matter what kind of a heart is associated with it, still it has power to choose in any direction. However wicked the heart, however intense its hatred of God and love of sin, the will can at any moment accept Christ and secure pardon and salvation. On the other hand, however good the heart, however intense its love of God and hatred of sin, the will can at any moment embrace sin, and hurl defiance in the face of God.

Holding such views of the 'fearful power of the will', Arminians must reject the doctrine of the certainty of a Christian's salvation. There is nothing that can make it certain, for the reason that the will is absolute in its power, and it is always uncertain. It may always choose, and is always liable to choose, either of two opposite destinies.

Some Christians have a happy faculty of believing whatever suits their taste. They accept some of the Arminian doctrines and reject others. They travel with Arminius up to the doctrine of 'falling from grace', and then they part company with him and seek the society of Calvin. They will not hear of God's making it certain by a decree of election that a given number of Christians will exercise faith in Christ and be saved; but they are perfectly willing that something shall make it certain that after the sinner has once accepted Christ he should never be parted from him. Such persons may be excellent Christians, but they are poor logicians.

II. The Calvinistic View of Perseverance

The Calvinistic view is thus stated by Calvin himself in the French *Confession of Faith:*

We believe that faith is not given to the elect only to introduce them into the right way, but also to make them continue in it to the end. For as it is God who hath begun the work, he will also perfect it.

This view is presented a little more elaborately in the *Westminster Confession:*

They whom God hath accepted in his Beloved, effectually called and sanctified by his Spirit, can neither totally nor finally fall away from the state of grace; but shall certainly persevere therein to the end, and be eternally saved.

It is easy to see which is the best doctrine. Arminians teach that I may be a child of God today and a child of the devil tomorrow, and that where I am to spend eternity remains a matter of uncertainty until soul and body separate.

Calvinists teach that the moment I put my soul with a trembling trust into the keeping of Christ, that moment I settle the question of my soul's happy destiny once for all; that I am henceforth just as safe in the kingdom of grace on earth as I will be hereafter in the kingdom of glory in heaven; that the same wisdom, power, and love are exercised on my behalf here and now as will be exercised on my behalf there and then; that the Good Shepherd will no more suffer me to stray beyond the limits of safety on this side of death than on the other side; that the greater the danger the greater his watchfulness, the greater my weakness the more constant his protection.

There are some doctrines which we believe only because constrained by the teachings of Scripture, such as, for example, the doctrine of eternal punishment. But this doctrine of the certain salvation of all who are born again, of all who once really embrace Christ, is one which all must be willing to believe. The only question is, Are we authorized to believe it? It seems clear to me that both reason and Scripture warrant such a belief.

1. *Look at the matter first in the light of reason. Why should God begin the work unless he means to carry it on to completion?*

Our Saviour bids us to sit down and count the cost, and not to begin an undertaking unless we are able to finish it (*Luke* 14:28). If such a course is discretion in us, is it not equally discretion in him? If, as the Good Shepherd, he goes in search of his lost sheep, and after finding it is not able to bring it all the way home, must leave it by the wayside to perish, does he not give his enemies reason to deride him? If, as the Divine Physician, he enters upon the treatment of a sin-sick soul, and after bringing it to a state of convalescence must suffer it to relapse and perish, does he not bring discredit on his profession? We can but ask, why should he seek the lost and partially save him, if his labour is to come to naught? Why should he invite the confidence of the dying sinner, and begin the curative process, if perfect restoration is not to result?

It might be answered that Christ does not make the beginning; that he waits for the sinner. His attitude, it may be said, is always that of a waiting Saviour. He merely receives those who come, and keeps them while they wish to stay. As the sinner's will, after conversion as before, is always uncontrolled and uncontrollable, it is ever uncertain how long any given sinner who comes to Christ will stay.

Even granting that this is a true view of the Saviour's attitude, we still can see no reason why he should receive a sinner, honour him with his friendship, bestow upon him his name, admit him to the number of God's children, make him an heir of God and a joint heir with himself, have the angels rejoicing over him, yet all the while knowing that the whole transaction would prove farcical; that in a little while this so greatly honoured sinner would be an alien from God, and again under the power of the devil.

Suppose a wealthy man takes a homeless little waif from the street, adopts him into his family, gives him his name, and makes him a joint heir with his own son to all of his property. You congratulate the fortunate little waif, and you praise his noble and generous benefactor. Whereupon he assures you that all that has been done must by-and-by be undone, for he knows with an infallible prevision that the object of his benefaction will prove unworthy, at length become unbearable, and he shall be constrained to divest him of all these honours and emoluments, and set him adrift as he found him. In such a case would you not ask in amazement why he had gone through with such an elaborate form of conferring a blessing when in the end no blessing was to be conferred? Can you think of any answer to the question? If we only allow foreknowledge to God, the final apostasy of any of his children seems highly improbable, for the reason that we cannot conceive that he would adopt a child, knowing at the time that he must afterwards cast him out.

But we do not believe for one moment that our Saviour's attitude is that of waiting. 'He seeks and saves the lost' (cf. *Luke* 19:10). He goes into the wilderness after his wandering sheep. He begins with the sinner, and the beginning is the guarantee of the end. To begin and not to complete would imply one of two things—change of mind or want of ability. No one will impute to him change of mind. 'He is the same yesterday, today, and forever' (*Heb.* 13:8). 'Having loved his own . . . he loved them to the end' (*John* 13:1).

Will anyone impute to him want of ability? This is practically what Arminianism does. Arminian writers teach that Christ cannot certainly keep the child of God from apostatizing without destroying his free will, and so robbing his conduct of all moral quality. When, therefore, Christ begins the work and fails to finish, the failure is due practically to Christ's inability to control the sinner's will. But Christ foreknew his inability, and therefore foreknew his failure, and hence it is unaccountable that he ever should have begun.

We cannot, however, concede Christ's inability. Not only does reason teach us that he who has power to transform the nature can control the will, but the Scriptures explicitly assert the very ability that is called in question. Paul writes to the Romans that God 'is of power to stablish you according to my gospel' (*Rom.* 16:25). Jude ascribes praise 'unto him that is able to keep you from falling, and to present you faultless before the presence of his glory with exceeding joy' (*Jude* 24). He who wrote the Epistle to the Hebrews declares that Jesus 'is able also to save them to the uttermost that come unto God by him' (*Heb.* 7:25). Surely he could not save them to the uttermost if he could not certainly save them to the end of this short life.

We can conceive of no motive that God could have in regenerating a sinner unless he thereby meant to save him. It is only the completion of the work that is to glorify God and exhibit his wisdom and his grace. It is not what we are, but what we shall be, when he shall present us before his Father's throne, 'not having spot nor wrinkle, nor any such thing', that is to reflect honour on our divine Saviour. But for that glorious consummation he could have no motive to begin with us. No artist would begin a great picture if he knew his work must be destroyed before finished. Only the completed work shows the genius of the artist and brings reward for labour.

2. *But we gladly turn to Scripture.*

(1) *What is the good work which God has begun in the Christian?*

It is regeneration, a new birth, the beginning of a new life. What do the Scriptures teach us as to the duration of this life? Suppose we were to find such texts as these in the Bible: 'He that believeth in me hath a life that shall continue a thousand years.' 'My sheep follow me, and I give unto them a life that shall last a thousand years.' 'The wages of sin is death, but the gift of God is a life that shall endure a thousand years.' 'Whosoever liveth and believeth on me, shall live a thousand years.' Would we not say that the word of God promised a thousand years of life to all who trust in Christ? Should we not say, if the life beginning with faith in Christ should end before the expiration of a thousand years, the promise had failed? Put the one word 'eternal' in the place of 'a thousand years', and is not the reasoning equally valid? But such substitution converts all the supposed texts into *bona fide* Scripture. The very name of the good work begun in the Christian implies the perpetuity of it.

(2) *The continuance of the good work is assured by the continual intercession of Christ.*

'He is able also to save them to the uttermost them who come unto God through him, seeing he ever liveth to make intercession for them' (*Heb.* 7:25) Christ prays for all his people, and him 'the Father heareth always' (cf. *John* 11:42). As long as he prays for them they are safe. 'Yes, provided they do not give up their faith.' But that is the very object of the intercession. When Christ would keep Peter from falling away and perishing, he prayed for him that his faith might not fail, and it did not fail (*Luke* 22:31-32). 'Ye are kept by the power of God through faith unto salvation' (*1 Pet.* 1:5). He who bestows the gift of faith at the first can continue it, and so keep his people by keeping their faith from failing.

(3) *The continuance of the good work is guaranteed in the covenant between Father and Son.*

Christ represents himself as dying for those who had been given to him of the Father: 'I lay down my life for the sheep' (*John* 10:15). 'My Father which gave them me is greater than all' (*John* 10:29). Christ prays, not for the world, but for those whom God has given him out of the world (*John* 17:9). Now, if all those who believe are given of the Father, and if Christ died for them with the covenant stipulation that they should have everlasting life, then God must make the promise good. This he will certainly do. When others rejected Christ, he comforted his heart with the assurance, 'All that the Father giveth me shall come to me . . . and this is the Father's will, that of all which he hath given me I should lose nothing, but should raise it up again at the last day' (*John* 6:37, 39).

(4) *The beginning of the good work is the difficult part.*

The first thing is to reconcile us to God, and this must be done by the death of his Son. 'Christ hath once suffered for sins, the just for the unjust, that he might bring us to God' (*1 Pet.* 3:18). This was the great work of Christ as measured by suffering and sacrifice. Yet he must do this before there could be even the beginning of a good work within us. What remains after this is comparatively easy. Hence the apostle argues: 'If, when we were enemies, we were reconciled to God by the death of his Son; much more, being reconciled, we shall be saved by his life' (*Rom.* 5:10). Having done the great thing for us even before we were his children, he will not fail, now that we are his children, to do the small remainder.

(5) *Finally, the Scriptures expressly state that the beginning and end of salvation are linked together by the immutable purpose of God.*

'Whom he did foreknow, he also did predestinate to be conformed to the image of his Son . . . Moreover, whom he did predestinate, them he also called: and whom he called, them he also justified; and whom he justified, them he also glorified' (*Rom.* 8:29-30). Here are five links in the golden chain of salvation.

The first link is *foreknowledge*. That lies back in eternity.

The second link is *predestination*. That also lies back in eternity. These two are always linked together: 'for whom he did foreknow, he also did predestinate.'

The third link is *effectual calling*. This belongs to time.

> Effectual calling is the work of God's Spirit, whereby, convincing us of our sin and misery, enlightening our minds in the knowledge of Christ, and renewing our wills, he doth persuade and enable us to embrace Jesus Christ, freely offered to us in the gospel. (*Westminster Shorter Catechism* Q.&A. 31.)

This is always linked with predestination: 'Moreover, whom he did predestinate, them he also called.'

The fourth link is *justification*. This also belongs to time.

> Justification is an act of God's free grace, wherein he pardoneth all our sins, and accepteth us as righteous in his sight, only for the righteousness of Christ imputed to us, and received by faith alone.'

This is always linked with the calling: 'Whom he called, them he also justified. (*Westminster Shorter Catechism* Q.&A. 33.)

The fifth link is *glorification*. This begins with the soul's entrance into heaven. It is always linked with justification: 'Whom he justified, them he also glorified.'

Having scanned this golden chain from beginning to end, and noted how link is coupled to link by the purpose and power of God, the apostle triumphantly exclaims: 'What shall we then say to these things? If God be for us, who can be against us?' (*Rom.* 8:31) Higher and higher does Paul lift his note of triumph, until he ends with the grand climax, beyond which the faith of assurance cannot go: 'I am persuaded that neither death, nor life, nor angels, nor principalities, nor powers, nor things present, nor things to come, nor height, nor depth, nor any other creature, shall be able to separate us from the love of God, which is in Christ Jesus our Lord' (*Rom.* 8:38-39). We are fully of Paul's persuasion, and in this persuasion we can understand why 'there is joy in the presence of the angels of God over one sinner that repenteth' (*Luke* 15:10). It means a soul added to the white-robed throng who cease not to praise God day and night, for ever and ever. The tear of penitence is the infallible prophecy that by-and-by—

> A new harp shall be strung,
> > and a new song shall be given,
> To the breezes which float
> > o'er the gardens of heaven.

7

CALVINISM TESTED BY LOVE

And we have known and believed the love that
God hath to us. God is love; and he that dwelleth
in love dwelleth in God, and God in him.
1 John 4:16

*D*oes Calvinism square with 'God's love'? If not, away with it. Does Calvinism obscure this truth? If so, it is so far false. We have no friendly entertainment for any theology that throws a shadow across the face of God; that puts a frown where we long to see a smile. The Bible leads us across forty centuries of human history, every page of which is darkened by man's wickedness and illumined by God's goodness. It leaves us looking

99

on man redeemed and glorified, and God wiping all tears from weeping eyes. The God of the Bible has a heart great enough for all the world, and gracious enough for the chief of sinners. Does Calvinism mar the loveliness of the inspired picture? Does it chill the warmth of his love, or limit the breadth of his sympathy? Does it shut the door of deliverance in the face of those whom divine love is inviting to enter? Does it make the gate straiter and the way narrower than the adorable Saviour has made them? If Calvinism cannot stand the test of love, let the verdict go against it.

We had rather murder logic than even to wound love. Love is the fountain from which redemption flows. It is the basis of our hopes and the life of our faith. It is the inspiration of our service and the breath of our prayers. It is our shade by day and our defence by night. It is our comfort in sorrow and our support in death. It is our supreme reason for joy here, and affords the only prospect of eternal joy hereafter. We cannot, therefore, defend a system that restricts the scope or cools the ardour of God's love. Away forever with any enemy that would narrow down, or in any manner impoverish, our confidence in that love. If Calvinism asks us to worship a God whose essential nature can be expressed by any other word than love, let us quickly and vehemently say, 'Get thee hence, Satan; for it is written, Thou shalt worship the Lord thy God, and him only shalt thou serve' (*Matt.* 4:10).

Calvinism divides the whole race of sinners into two classes, the elect and the non-elect. The elect include all those who have been, and who shall be, saved. The non-elect include all those who have died, or who shall hereafter die, unsaved.

I. GOD's LOVE FOR THE ELECT

No one will accuse Calvinism of withholding the full benefit of divine love from the elect. Calvin and his followers teach that God has from eternity loved his elect people, and cherished the invincible purpose of saving them from sin and hell. In the execution of this purpose, he sends his Son to die for them; he gives them the knowledge of his grace through the gospel; he offers them life on condition of faith and repentance; he secures the fulfilment of the condition by sending his Spirit to regenerate them; he makes them to persevere in the way of life by working in them to will and to do of his good pleasure. The only limit to the exercise of God's love in behalf of the elect is the limit of their need. He foreknows them, predestinates them, calls them, justifies them, and glorifies them.

In the parable of the lost sheep we have a picture of Calvinistic salvation (*Luke* 15:4-7). The shepherd went after his sheep till he found it; then he laid it on his shoulder, rejoicing, and carried it home. Here was ample love. It did all that was needed to make the rescue of the sheep an absolute certainty. It was love's eyes that sought and found it; it was love's hands that lifted it tenderly to the shepherd's shoulders; it was love's strength that bore it safe to the fold. No one can find fault with such love as being too meagre. This parable is the picture of Christ saving a sinner in a truly Calvinistic manner. He both seeks and saves the lost. His eyes of love search out the sinner; his hands of love lay hold upon him, and sweetly constrain him to yield; and on the broad shoulders of his love he bears the sinner home. How much did love do for the dead and buried Lazarus? It wept at his grave; it cried aloud, 'Lazarus, come forth'; it imparted the life that heard and obeyed. If love does thus much for the sinner, 'dead in trespasses and sins', no one can reproach it for not doing more. That miracle is a Calvinistic picture of Christ saving a sinner. His love yearns over the dead, speaks to the dead, and imparts the life that hears and obeys. Love can go no further, can do no more than God's love in Christ has done and is doing for the salvation of his elect.

> 'Twas the same love that spread the feast,
>   That sweetly forced us in;
> Else we had still refused to taste,
>   And perished in our sin.

It is, indeed, objected to Calvinism, that in the case of the elect it magnifies too much the agency of divine love; that it exalts the love of God at the expense of the freedom of the sinner's will. Calvinism, it is said, represents God as saving the sinner without asking his consent. Does he belong to the number of the elect? Then, will he, nill he, the love of God lays hold of him and saves him; it does not pause to parley with him.

The adversaries of Calvinism would not press the parable of the lost sheep quite so far. To make it a true picture of the divine agency in saving sinners, they would represent the shepherd as pausing when he draws near enough for the sheep to hear his voice, and calling to it. If the sheep will not hearken and come to him, then it must take the consequences and perish.

We think the Calvinistic picture truer to Scripture, and all must admit that it brings the love of God into greater prominence. None can question that, so far as the elect are concerned, Calvinism lays a tremendous emphasis on the love of God. Their salvation, from first to last, is the fruit of love. Through all the endless future, redeemed sinners will find no explanation of the blessedness which they enjoy other than the love which glowed in the heart of God before the foundations of the world were laid.

II. GOD'S LOVE FOR THE UNSAVED

With reference to the unsaved, what is the doctrine of Calvinism? This question is the crucial test of the system. It smiles benignantly on the elect, but it is supposed to wear a very harsh and forbidding aspect when it turns its face toward the unsaved. If this be true, if it have no pity in its heart for the incorrigible sinners who destroy themselves, we are ready to say that it is not of God. Christ wept tears of compassion while looking on the sinners who had sinned away their day of grace. If Calvinism have not the spirit of Christ, it is none of his (*Rom.* 8:9). It professes to find its chief supporter in Christ. It can only make good this profession by showing a love as broad and a sympathy as tender as his. What can we say on its behalf?

We can say that Calvinism puts no limit whatever on the love of God. It limits the number of the saved, but it does not restrict the love of God to the saved. It limits the application of the benefits of redemption, but it does not ascribe this limitation to the want of love. It accepts John 3:16 in all its length and breadth: 'God so loved the world, that he gave his only begotten Son, that whosoever believeth in him should not perish.' Calvin is good authority with all Calvinists, and his comment on this text is as follows:

> Christ brought life, because the heavenly Father loves the human race, and wishes that they should not perish. He employed the universal term *whosoever,* both to invite indiscriminately all to partake of life, and to cut off every excuse from unbelievers. Such, also, is the import of the term *world.* Though there is nothing in the world that is worthy of God's favour, yet he shows himself to be reconciled to the whole world when he invites all men, without exception, to the faith of Christ.

The Synod of Dort, called the 'grim synod', because of the rigidity of its Calvinism, was careful not to bound the love of God by the decree of election.

> As many as are called by the gospel are unfeignedly called; for God doth most earnestly and truly declare in his word what will be acceptable to him,

namely, that all who are called should comply with the invitation, He, moreover, promises seriously eternal life and rest to as many as shall come to him and believe on him. It is not the fault of the gospel, nor of Christ offered therein, nor of God, who calls men by the gospel, and confers upon them various gifts, that those who are called by the ministry of the word refuse to come and be converted. The fault lies in themselves.

This declaration represents the belief of all the great Calvinistic churches of the Reformation period, and it plainly implies that they held and taught that God's love is world-wide and race-embracing. They do not modify nor dilute the broadest statements of the word of God touching his gracious readiness to receive all sinners, without exception, on the ground of their faith and penitence, to the arms of his forgiving love.

We may well inquire in what respect Calvinism comes short of its rival theologies in exhibiting the love of God toward the lost. We have seen that it far surpasses them in the weight of emphasis which it puts on the love of God toward the saved. Does it fall equally far behind them in the measure of love which it represents God as manifesting toward those who are not saved?

According to the view of evangelical Arminians, what measure of love does God manifest towards those who are finally lost? Is it not correct to say that all that God does is to provide an atonement sufficient for them, to offer it sincerely and freely to them, and to give them grace to enable them to accept if they will? This is the whole process. God's love does not effect their salvation; it merely provides a salvation and offers it to them, but leaves them, despite the enabling grace conferred, to reject it and be lost. What greater love is represented here than is contained in the deliverance of the Synod of Dort? Touching the extent of the atonement, the synod says:

> The death of the Son of God is the only most perfect sacrifice and satisfaction for sin; is of infinite worth and value, abundantly sufficient to expiate the sins of the whole world.

Touching the extent of the offer, they say:

> The promise of the gospel is that whosoever believeth in Christ crucified shall not perish, but have everlasting life. This promise, together with the command to repent and believe, ought to be declared and published to all nations, and to all persons, promiscuously and without distinction, to whom God, out of his good pleasure, sends the gospel. And whereas many who are called by the gospel do not repent, nor

believe in Christ, but perish in unbelief, this is not owing to any defect or insufficiency in the sacrifice offered by Christ upon the cross, but is wholly to be imputed to themselves.

Thus, it is seen that Calvinism exhibits the same all-sufficient atonement, and makes the same sincere and indiscriminate offer. Is it suggested that Arminianism has the advantage in that it represents God as bestowing upon those that are lost grace sufficient to enable them to accept the offered salvation if they will? Calvinism is ready to say as much. This same Synod of Dort says that, in addition to giving to those who 'refuse to come and be converted' a sincere offer of salvation, God 'confers upon them various gifts'. Calvinists believe that God gives his Holy Spirit to those who resist the gracious invitations of the gospel, and who finally perish in their sins. While they believe in invincible grace, they also believe in resistible grace; and this latter answers to the full measure of the 'common sufficient grace' of the Arminian teaching.

How, then, do the two systems compare? The Arminian says that God manifests his love to all sinners, the saved and the unsaved, by providing an atonement sufficient for all, by offering it freely to all, and by giving grace sufficient, and yet not in such measure as certainly decides any sinner to accept salvation. The love of God actually saves no soul; it makes the salvation of no soul absolutely certain; it merely puts salvation within the reach of all if they will to accept it. Now, the Calvinist can consistently say that the love of God does that much for the lost. He is not restrained by the logical necessity of his system from teaching that the love of God does as much for the non-elect as the Arminian represents it as doing for all. Without doing any violence to the principles of his creed, the Calvinist can say that God did as much for Judas Iscariot as the Arminian is willing to say that he did for John the apostle.

All parties among Christians are confronted with this somewhat startling dilemma: God is either not willing or not able to save all sinners. If the former, where is his benevolence? If the latter, where is his omnipotence? Suppose we say that God is not able to save *all;* then the logical conclusion is that he is not able to save *any.* Manifestly, the same problem is involved in every case. The power that could raise Lazarus could raise all dead men. So, if God were able to quicken one dead sinner into life, he must be able to quicken all. One sinner is not deader than another. Shall we say that God cannot save sinners? That his power exhausts itself in making it possible for sinners to save themselves if they will? To quote the language of Dr R. L. Dabney,

> Shall we so exalt the prerogatives of a fancied free will as to strip God of his omnipotence over sinful free agents?

If so, then we have no solid foundation for our hopes, either in this life, or that which is to come. If God cannot save sinners, neither can he keep them saved; for the same problem is still involved, that of exercising control over free, self-determining wills. If he cannot keep them saved, heaven may be only a temporary home for those who die in the faith. Again we may use the language of our great theologian, and say that

> this theory undermines the hope of every sinner in the world, and spreads a pall of fear and uncertainty over heaven itself.

We cannot endure this horn of the dilemma. Let us try the other.

God is able to save all, but is not willing. This seems a hard saying; who can bear it? Calvinists are bound to bear it. They stand or fall by God's sovereignty. If the doctrine of God's absolute control over all his creatures and over all their actions involves consequences which they are not willing to face, then they must abandon the field in defeat. They must stand to the statement that God could save all sinners if only he would purpose to do so. True Calvinists most firmly believe that the potter, who has 'power over the clay, of the same lump to make one vessel unto honour, and another unto dishonour' (*Rom.* 9:21), has power to make all the vessels unto honour. That he does not make all unto honour is not owing to inability. To what, then, is it owing? Are we shut up to the necessity of saying that it is owing to the want of benevolence? Suppose we let Paul explain. 'What if God, willing to show his wrath, and to make his power known, endured with much long-suffering the vessels of wrath fitted to destruction: and that he might make known the riches of his glory on the vessels of mercy, which he had afore prepared unto glory?' (*Rom.* 9:22-23).

We must not fail to notice that no agency is ascribed to God in fitting the vessels of wrath to destruction. He finds them fitted. He finds no other kind. The vessels of mercy 'were by nature the children of wrath, even as others'. Both kinds of vessels were clay 'of the same lump'. What did God do toward saving the vessels of wrath? He 'endured them with much long-suffering'. Does not this show tenderness and compassion? Why did he not do more toward their salvation? Because he was 'willing to show his wrath, and to make known his power'. He saw it best, after exhibiting his long-suffering patience and his gracious readiness to pardon them on condition of penitence, to leave some sinners to reap the just rewards of their iniquity, in order that he might thus display his wrath against sin, and demonstrate his power to deal with it as it deserves. He does these sinners no wrong, simply permits them to work out their own destruction; but at the same time he furnishes a lesson to the universe on the hatefulness of sin, and the stable foundation on which the kingdom of holiness rests, notwithstanding the efforts of wicked men and of devils to destroy it.

If such a course seems best in reference to some sinners, why not in reference to all, as they are all in the same condemnation, 'clay of the same lump'? Because God wishes to 'make known the riches of his glory', and to this end he makes some vessels of mercy, 'preparing them afore unto glory'. We may say, in a word, that when God looked upon the lump of sinful humanity he decided to deal with it in the way which would best serve the purpose of displaying all the attributes of his glorious character, and thus promote the highest ends of his moral government. He might destroy the whole lump; he might transform the whole lump; or he might divide it, and make some vessels unto honour, and others to dishonour. His justice calls for the first course; his benevolence calls for the second; his wisdom calls for the third. By this course he illustrates both his justice and benevolence, and at the same time secures the highest ends of his unerring wisdom. In the case of those who are lost, God permits their self-destruction despite the entreaties of his benevolence. In the case of the saved, God, by the invincible power of his grace, rescues them despite the demands of his justice. In the case of both classes, the compassionate Christ is 'over all, God blessed for evermore' (*Rom.* 9:5).

If this explanation be unsatisfactory, it is, possibly, because we have not grasped, in all its bearings, the great truth that salvation is all of grace, and that it can, therefore, be no reflection on any attribute of God's perfect character if he decline to put forth his saving power on behalf of any given sinner, or number of sinners. Grant that God can save sinners, and yet does not, still this is nothing against his benevolence, unless sinners have some kind of claim on him.

If we cannot rest in Paul's solution of God's discriminating mercy, perhaps we might find rest in

Christ's. Why does God hide the things of salvation from one class, and reveal them unto another? Is it because he cannot reveal them unto both classes? No, it is 'even so, Father; for so it seemed good in thy sight' (*Matt.* 11:25-26).

III. CALVINISM AND THE PROMISES OF THE GOSPEL

Calvinism does not rob a promise or an invitation of the gospel of the slightest fraction of its preciousness. 'Ho, everyone that thirsteth, come ye to the waters, and he that hath no money; come ye, buy, and eat; yea, come, buy wine and milk without money and without price' (*Isa.* 55:1). Who does not rejoice in the breadth of this love and in the warmth of this solicitude? No Calvinist but would delight to shout this gracious message in the ears of every thirsty soul on earth. We believe that the offer is in good faith, and that the promise will be fulfilled to all who accept it. We believe that, while many will not accept, many will accept under the sweet and gracious and effectual drawings of God.

'Whosoever will, let him take the water of life freely' (*Rev.* 22:17). Calvinism does not hedge any away from the fountain by a secret decree of God. The only barrier keeping any away is the sinner's perverse will. 'Ye will not come' is the statement of Christ (*John* 5:40). The only effect of God's decree of election is to overcome this suicidal obduracy of will, and while the invitations of grace are extended, thousands, drawn of God, accept them. If any will come without this drawing, they are heartily welcome. The promise holds good to the last syllable. Whosoever believeth shall not perish. 'Him that cometh unto me I will in no wise cast out' (*John* 6:37).

As a matter of fact, Calvinistic preachers have proclaimed as broad a gospel as any other evangelical preachers. Who has gone beyond Bunyan in the picture which he draws of the first offer of salvation to the Jerusalem sinners, the murderers of Christ?

'Repent everyone of you; be baptized every one of you in his name for the remission of sins; and you shall, everyone of you, receive the gift of the Holy Ghost' [*Acts* 2:38].

'But I was one of them that plotted to take away his life. May I be saved by him?'—EVERY ONE OF YOU.

'But I was one of them that bare false witness against him. Is there grace for me?'—FOR EVERY ONE OF YOU.

'But I was one of them that cried out, crucify him! crucify him! and desired that Barabbas, the murderer, might live rather than him. What will become of me, think you?'—I am to preach repentance and remission of sins TO EVERY ONE OF YOU.

'But I was one of them that did spit in his face when he stood before his accusers; I also was one that mocked him when, in anguish, he hung bleeding on the tree. Is there room for me?'—FOR EVERY ONE OF YOU . . .

'But I railed on him; I reviled him; I hated him; I rejoiced to see him mocked at by others. Can there be hopes for me?'—There is, FOR EVERY ONE OF YOU.[1]

I doubt if any preacher, of any age, has been more firm in his adherence to Calvinism, or more persistent in proclaiming it, than Charles H. Spurgeon. He fairly exulted in the championship of all the distinctive doctrines of this system. Yet who ever preached a broader or more hope-inspiring gospel than he? In one of his sermons on election, in which he presents the doctrine without the slightest apology, he takes occasion to say:

[1] John Bunyan, *The Jerusalem Sinner Saved* (Edinburgh: Banner of Truth, 2005) pp. 10-11, emphasis added.

Some of you have listened to my voice these ten years. I ask you if you have ever heard me utter a single sentence which at all contradicts the doctrine of God's great goodness? You may have so construed it by mistake, but no such teaching has passed my lips. Do I not, again and again, assert the universal benevolence of God—the infinite and overflowing goodness of the heart of the Most High? If any man can preach on the great text, 'God is love', though I may not be able to preach with the same eloquence, I will venture to vie with him in the decision, heartiness, delight, earnestness and plainness with which he may expound his theme, be he who he may, or what he may. There is not the slightest shadow of a conflict between God's sovereignty and God's goodness.

It may be said that when Calvinists preach an unrestricted gospel they sacrifice logic to love, that their hearts are better than their heads, that their preaching is broader than their creed. This should, at any rate, be said with some modesty, seeing the accusation stands against the preachers who made the deepest impression on the age in which they lived, and left the most illustrious names which history transmits to succeeding ages. What names of the seventeenth century shine with such bright radiance as those of Baxter, Bunyan, and Rutherford? Of the eighteenth century as those of Edwards, Whitefield, and the Erskines? Of the nineteenth as those of Chalmers, M'Cheyne, and Spurgeon? We let Spurgeon speak in defence of them all.

> I have preached here, you know it, invitations as free as those which proceeded from the lips of Master John Wesley. Van Armin himself, the founder of the Arminian school, could not more honestly have pleaded with the very vilest of the vile to come to Jesus than I have done. Have I therefore felt in my mind that there was a contradiction here? No, nothing of the kind; because I know it to be my duty to sow beside all waters, and like the sower in the parable to scatter the seed on the stony ground, as well as upon the good ground, knowing that election does not narrow the gospel call, which is universal, but only affects the effectual call, which is, and must be, particular. My business is to give the general call — the Holy Spirit will see to its application to the chosen.

Calvinism is not more the fruit of logic than of loyalty to Scripture. Calvinism can never escape the logical necessity of putting the sinner's will under the control of God, or denying sovereignty to God. But it cannot deny sovereignty to God without discarding Scripture, and teaching that prayer is folly. It cannot exempt the sinner's will from God's control without ruling God out of history, and making prophecy an impossibility. It cannot ascribe foreknowledge to God without believing in the absolute certainty of future events. But Calvinism holds these positions not more in deference to the demands of sound logic than in deference to the more imperative demands of Scripture. Calvinism, therefore, is only true to itself when it preaches the whole word of God, without qualification or mental reservation.

IV. God's Love for the Unlovable

Calvinism especially emphasizes the love of God in that it represents the objects of his love as utterly unlovable.

Recently a distinguished preacher of the Methodist Church remarked to me that he thought the doctrine of entire sanctification, as taught by its recent advocates, bore a much closer affinity to Calvinism than to Arminianism. 'How do you account for the fact', I asked, 'that it spread so readily among the Methodist churches, and can get no foothold in Presbyterian churches?' He replied that he had tried to explain the fact and had been unable. Whereupon, I suggested that if the people were once indoctrinated with the Calvinistic idea of the utterly loathsome and deadly nature of sin, they could never be convinced that it was possible to get rid of it by any such easy and sudden process as that offered by the holiness brethren. He admitted that this was probably the true explanation.

Undoubtedly Calvinism brands sin with a deeper infamy than any other school of theology. By as much as it emphasizes the hatefulness of sin, by so much does it emphasize the love of God, of which sinners are the object. God does not wait for any improvement in sinners before loving them. 'God commendeth his love toward us in that while we were yet sinners Christ died for us' (*Rom.* 5:8). He does not confer enabling grace and then wait for us to turn unto him before conferring the gift of life. 'But God who is rich in mercy, for his great love wherewith he loved us, even when we were dead in sins, hath quickened us together with Christ' (*Eph.* 2:4-5). The love of God did not merely pity us and provide a way to save us, but it lavished upon us all the infinite wealth of salvation. Before we were born, when as yet we existed only in the purpose and foreknowledge of God, his love put our names in the book of life, furnished a ransom for our guilt, a robe to cover our iniquity, and

made ready a place for us at the marriage supper
of the Lamb.

Dr John Newton was fond of telling of an old lady
in his church at Olney, who said: 'It is well for me that
God chose me for his own before I was born; for if
he had not, he would never have seen any reason for
doing so afterward.' That is just the respect wherein
Calvinism exalts the love of God. His amazing love
does not wait to see a reason. He loves us without a
reason and against all reason, except the one reason,
'God is love' (*1 John* 4:8). He can no more help loving than the sun can help shining.

> Grander than ocean's story,
> Or songs of forest trees—
> Purer than breath of morning
> Or evening's gentle breeze—
> Clearer than mountain echoes
> Ring out from peaks above—
> Rolls on the glorious anthem
> Of God's eternal love.
>
> Dearer than any lovings
> The truest friends bestow;
> Stronger than all the yearnings
> A mother's heart can know;
> Deeper than earth's foundation
> And far above all thought;
> Broader than heav'n's high arches
> The love that Christ has brought.

8

CALVINISM TESTED BY FRUIT

Wherefore by their fruits ye shall know them.
Matthew 7:20

*W*e have been looking at the creed of Calvin in a series of studies to see if it is logical and scriptural. It so commends itself to us. But many think differently. Many denounce it as an outrage on reason, and a 'disgrace to theology', charging that it is based on such a perversion of Scripture as is grossly dishonouring to God. Is there any way by which we can further demonstrate its truth or its falseness? Yes: we can apply the most trustworthy of all tests. 'Grapes do not grow on thorns, nor figs on thistles' (cf. *Matt.* 7:16). I hold in my hand a seed.

Is it apple or pear? Plant it, and the fruit will settle the question beyond all controversy. Calvinism has been planted. It has sprung up and brought fruit. This fruit is preserved in history. It is easy to inspect it and judge of its quality.

We will not go back to the apostolic church, nor to the church immediately succeeding the days of the apostles. We believe that the apostles and their immediate successors were Calvinists of the deepest dye. How could John have escaped Calvinism after listening to the discourses of Christ which he records in the sixth and tenth chapters of his Gospel? How could Paul have written the eighth and ninth of Romans, the first of Ephesians, and, in fact, all his other epistles, unless he had been a Calvinist? How could anyone but a rank Calvinist ever have preached such a sermon as Peter preached on the day of Pentecost? (See especially *Acts* 2:23.)

But as plain as all this is to us, inasmuch as others cannot see it and will not admit it, we do not point you to the primitive church to show you the fruits of Calvinism in its widespread triumphs and heroic sufferings. We will confine ourselves to a period in the history of the church when, by the admission of all, whatever was wrought for God and humanity in the Protestant church was wrought by Calvinism.

From the time that Luther shook the foundation of the papacy by proclaiming the doctrine of 'justification by faith alone', Calvinism had the field against Rome all to itself for nearly two hundred years. Its great rival had no existence in the Protestant church until 1616, and whatever power it exerted until the days of Wesley cannot be mentioned to its praise. The great battles between the spirit of inquiry and blind submission to authority, between liberty and tyranny, between light and darkness, had all been fought and won before Arminianism was strong enough to buckle on the armour. Evidently, the place to look for the genuine fruits of Calvinism is in the two centuries between Luther and John Wesley. Would you know Romanism? Look not at the church in this country, where there are so many influences modifying its product; but look at Italy, at South America, at Mexico. Rome can take to herself the credit of whatever there is to boast of in the intellectual, moral, and spiritual condition of those countries, for over them she has held exclusive sway sufficiently long for the fruits of her teaching to mature. For the same reason we go to the Reformation period and the century succeeding to find what the creed of Calvin planted in the soil of the human heart will produce in the way of individual and national character. The merest glance will show that the period to which we refer was not the glorious millennium of prophecy. The churches in revolt against Rome and flying the blue banner of Calvinism were not in any sense immaculate. But, making due allowance for the spirit of the age, for which these churches were in no large measure responsible, we are perfectly willing to point to the fruits which they bore, and let Calvinism stand or fall as judged by that test. What are some of the fruits?

I. PURITY OF MORALS.

One might easily suppose that Calvinism stands for a system of doctrine which could have little influence on practical life. The name suggests at once the profound deeps of the divine decrees, the unsearchable judgments of God, and his ways that are past finding out (cf. *Rom.* 11:33). How can human conduct be influenced by an inquiry into those things which are said to have transpired in the secret councils of eternity? We think there is a very clear answer to this how; but we are not now concerned about philosophy, but about facts. What was the influence of Calvinistic doctrine on Calvin himself? Perhaps you are ready to answer, 'It made him burn Servetus.' Hardly, for the papacy was not infected with Calvinism, and yet it was a famous burner of heretics. Candour must ascribe that sin of Calvin, not to the peculiarity of his doctrinal belief, but to the persecuting spirit of the age. Nearly every man of his day thought that God demanded the destruction of heretics. Calvin was just as ready to go to the stake himself for the glory of God as to send Servetus there.

Ernest Renan pronounces Calvin 'the most Christian man of his generation'. What was the influence of his teaching and life on Geneva? They made it the brightest spot on the map of Europe. John Knox said: 'Elsewhere the word of God is taught as purely, but never anywhere have I seen God obeyed as faithfully.' James Anthony Froude testifies that

> Calvinism, as it existed at Geneva, and as it has endeavoured to be wherever it took root for a century and a half after him, was not a system of opinions, but an attempt to make the will of God, as revealed in the Bible, an authoritative guide for social as well as for personal direction.

It is a familiar fact that the city of Geneva could not at first endure the severity of morals which Calvin had tried to enforce, and for this reason expelled him. He was soon recalled, however, and Geneva became an asylum for those who loved righteousness. Both his teaching and his spirit found a home in the hearts of the Puritans of England. Their name is the imperishable memorial of the scrupulous sanctity of their lives.

> They abhorred, as no body of men ever more abhorred, all conscious mendacity, all impurity, all moral wrong of every kind, so far as they could recognize it.

Thus speaks the great historian previously quoted, and he further says,

> Whatever exists at this moment in England and Scotland of conscientious fear of doing evil is the remnant of the convictions which were branded by the Calvinists into the people's hearts.

These same Calvinists, driven from their native land by the oppression of king and high church prelates, planted the seeds of their religious system in the virgin soil of New England. In this easy-going, self-indulgent age, it is deemed the proper thing to ridicule the old-time Puritanism of Massachusetts, and to refer with a shudder to the mythical blue laws of Connecticut; but no one can for a moment doubt that the face of Christendom would look much more like heaven, at least in the one matter of morals, of strict, unbending integrity, of rigid, uncompromising loyalty to God, if human conduct were today on as high a plane as it was placed by the Pilgrim fathers. Moreover, the salt which has not yet entirely lost its savour, and which is the chief influence in preserving our country from moral putrefaction, was brought to our shores by the vessels which brought the Puritans to New England, the Dutch Calvinists to New York and Pennsylvania, the Scotch-Irish to the Valley of Virginia, and the Huguenots to the Carolinas. Once again we quote from Froude: 'The first symptom of Calvinism, wherever it established itself, was to make the moral law the rule for states as well as nations.'

II. Heroism of Character.

We are not so foolish as to claim all heroism as the fruit of Calvinism. Every faith, however false and baneful, has its martyrs. But certainly one of the most direct effects of Calvinistic belief is to free the soul in which it finds lodgment from the fear of man, and to brace it for rendering unswerving allegiance to God.

The Calvinist believes that God is in every incident that touches his life; that every pain and every peril are of his appointment, and must, therefore, be encountered in the spirit of worship. Jesus called the bitter cup which was filled to the brim with the malice and cruelty of his relentless enemies 'the cup which my Father hath given me' (*John* 18:11); hence, he submissively drank it. Calvinism in its essence is just this recognition of God's will in every event of life, and it necessarily inspires heroic doing and suffering.

Luther's dauntless courage has been embalmed in a few pithy sentences with which nearly all the world is familiar. Being admonished not to go to Worms, where, it was thought, his enemies were plotting to take away his life, he said: 'If the devils were as numerous in Worms as the tiles on the housetops, I should not hesitate to leap in among them.' On another occasion, when warned not to put himself in the power of Duke George, he said: 'If it should rain Duke Georges for nine days, and each one should be nine times more fierce than the present one, I should go forward.'

Calvin was of the same mettle. Referring to the calumnies of his enemies, he says: 'But the devil, with all his hosts, is deceived if he think to overwhelm me with falsehoods, or to render me more timid, indolent, or dilatory by such indignities.'

Who is not familiar with the words spoken by the Regent Murray over the remains of Calvin's illustrious pupil, John Knox: 'Here lies one who never feared the face of man'?

These instances might be due to natural temperament. The demonstration is clearer if we find large bodies of men actuated by this faith, and displaying a like disregard of danger and death. We point to Cromwell and his famous Ironsides. They offered prayer on the eve of every battle, and entered the conflict chanting the psalms of David. Every man of them believed that he was a chosen instrument in the hands of God for the overthrow of tyranny. They never turned their backs on a foe.

We point to the great army of martyrs. While it is true, as already conceded, that every religion and every religious sect may boast its martyrs, it is also true that the great army of martyrs offered upon the altar of religious and civil liberty since the Reformation has been offered by the Calvinistic churches. We may pause only to mention the names of the Waldenses, the victims of the Spanish Inquisition in Italy and Spain, the massacre of St Bartholomew, the victims of Philip and Alva in Holland, of Bloody Mary in England, of Claverhouse in Scotland.

We are not concerned just now to inquire how this happened, but here is the fact as broad as the face of a whole century—when all the dearest interests of mankind were trembling in the balance, when they could only be purchased and preserved by the blood and ashes of a hundred thousand martyrs, the Calvinistic creed furnished the costly offering. We do not say that no other creed could furnish such an offering; we do say that no other creed has done it. When God needed an enthusiasm for liberty and a heroism for righteousness equal to the appalling task of acquiring these at the cost of tortures unspeakable, and of deaths innumerable, he suffered the Frenchman, John Calvin, to formulate the creed that was to inspire and sustain the enthusiasm and the heroism. When God suffers some of the critics of Calvin and Calvinism to achieve something equally glorious, then we will listen to their puerile criticisms with more patience.

III. ZEAL OF LIBERTY.

Calvinism prostrates the soul in helplessness before God, but it exalts it above slavish subjection to man. A republican church and a republican state took their rise about the same time in Geneva; and from that day to this Calvinism has ever been identified with the cause of liberty, or the rights of man. When left free it usually crystallizes itself into the form of a Presbyterian Church, as in Switzerland, France, Holland, Scotland, and in the Presbyterian churches of the United States. It must be more than a mere coincidence that Presbyterianism and Calvinism are usually in alliance. It must mean that Calvinism essentially tends to that form of government which guarantees the largest measure of liberty to the individual that is consistent with the order of the whole. It is the form of government, a representative republic, which the wisest statesmanship of modern times declares to be the best fitted for manifesting and preserving civil liberty. It was easy for the despotic James I of England to see that presbytery agrees with monarchy as well as God with the devil. Where Calvinism does not clothe itself in the garb of Presbyterianism, it takes the form of independency, as in the Congregational and Baptist Churches. It must always take a form that expresses its hostility to one-man power, and proclaims the doctrine of equality and brotherhood.

When we glance at the period in which we have agreed to confine our search for the fruits of Calvinism, what do we see? Wars are waging in France, in Holland, in England and in Scotland. Everywhere the prize at stake was the same—the right of man, as man, to life, liberty, and the pursuit of happiness. The deniers of this right in France were Catherine de Medici and 'her litter of hyena cubs', as Froude called them. The upholders of the right were the noble Coligny, and after him the chivalrous Henry of Navarre. The Calvinists were arrayed on the side of the latter.

In Holland it was Philip of Spain, the most bigoted, selfish, and cruel king of his age, and the bloody Duke of Alva, against William of Orange. The Calvinists fought under the latter. That little ragged sea coast, saved from the ocean by artificial sand banks, has committed to history one of the most marvellous records of unconquerable devotion to liberty, civil and religious, that any people has ever made. Motley writes,

It would be unjust and futile to detract from the vast debt that republic owed to the Genevan church. The fires which consumed the last vestige of royal and sacerdotal despotism throughout the independent republic had been lighted by the hands of Calvinists. Throughout the blood-stained soil of France, too, the men who were fighting the same great battle as were the Netherlands against Philip and the Inquisition, the valiant cavaliers of Dauphine and Provence, knelt on the ground before the battle, smote their iron breasts with their mailed hands, uttered a Calvinistic prayer, and then charged upon the Guise under the white plume of the Bearnese.

In England it was Charles and Laud on the side of arbitrary power against Cromwell, Hampden, and Pym, who stood for the rights of the people. The Puritans were with the latter.

In Scotland it was Mary Stuart against Murray and Knox. Everywhere the story is the same. The Calvinists were ever fighting for the right as against might, for the oppressed as against the oppressor.

When the youthful colonies of this country cast off the yoke of British rule, the Puritans of New England, the Dutch of the Middle States, the Scotch-Irish and Huguenots of the Southern States joined hands to secure the liberties which we today enjoy. The spirit of Calvin lived in all their hearts. The first declaration of independence was put forth by the Presbyterians of Mecklenburg, N.C.; and the first religious body to speak out in favour of separation from Great Britain was the Presbyterian Synod of Philadelphia.

How happened it that in all of the battles throughout the entire period to which our investigation is confined, for the enlargement of human rights and for the repression of despotic authorities, Calvinists should have taken the lead? A distinguished Arminian writer admits the fact, but says it was merely an accident of history. His words are:

> Position has often in history produced in all parties palpable violations of, and discordance with, their principles. Romanists often become, by position, asserters of ultra democracy, and Protestants of absolute despotism. And so Calvinism has historically been, by position, the advocate for revolution, and Arminianism the asserter of authority. In fact, as Arminianism has been, as above shown, the ruling doctrine of the church, and Calvinism an insurgent specialty, so the historical position of the first has been favourable to the assertion of authority, and the normal position of the latter has been revolt. This may be called one of the accidents of history.

So writes John F. Hurst in *Johnson's Encyclopedia*. The question is, How came Calvinism to occupy the position which made it the advocate of revolution? It occupied that position of its own accord.

This is just what we are reciting to its glory. It deliberately chose a position of revolt against tyranny, and smote it in the face with the fist of righteousness. Bishop Hurst shows by logic that is very conclusive to his own mind that Arminianism, judged by its principles, ought always to be the advocate of freedom; that Calvinism, judged by its principles, ought always to be the asserter of absolutism. But history shows, by the bishop's own concession, that the position of each of the parties has ever been exactly the opposite of its principles. How do you account for this contradiction of position to principle, bishop? 'Oh, it is merely one of the accidents of history.'

We reply that, if accidental at all, it is more than one of the accidents of history. It is an accident that keeps on repeating itself, and that with a uniformity that never varies, just as spring always succeeds to winter, and day to night. Bishop Hurst reminds us of Dr Sangrado, in *Gil Blas*. His only remedies were bleeding and potions of hot water. His patients usually died, but the doctor was able to ascribe this to merely an accident of history. 'If I was not so sure as I am of the principle on which I proceed, I should think that my remedies were pernicious in almost all the cases that come under my care.' Our good bishop is too sure of his principles to allow facts to bias his conclusions. Our historian, Bancroft, was not so invulnerable to the impact of historic evidence. He thought that there was something inherent in Calvinism which made it the foe of tyranny and the friend of man. His words are:

> On the banks of Lake Geneva, Calvin stood forth the boldest reformer of his day; not personally engaging in political intrigue, yet by promulgating great ideas forming the seed-plot of revolution; acknowledging no ordination but the choice of the laity, no patent of nobility but that of the elect of God with its seals of eternity. Wherever Calvinism came it created division; its symbol was a flaming sword. It was faithful to a religion without a prelate, and to a government without a king.

According to this high authority, the hostility of Calvinism to kingly prerogative was not accidental, it was the very breath of its life. Hence, he further says:

> He that will not honour the memory and respect the influence of Calvin knows but little of the origin of American liberty.

We cannot refrain from introducing another strong writer, Rufus Choate, a man of comprehensive and judicial mind. He says,

> I trace to Geneva as an influence on the English character, a new theology, new politics, another tone of character, the opening of another era of time and of liberty. I trace to it the great civil war in England, the republican constitution framed in the cabin of *The Mayflower,* the divinity of Jonathan Edwards, the battle of Bunker Hill, the independence of America.

The German historian, Ranke, is quoted as saying, 'Calvin is virtually the founder of America.' If history can be trusted to make anything a matter of certain knowledge, there can be no reasonable doubt that Motley is safe within the limits of truth when he writes: 'To the Calvinists, more than to any other class of men, the political liberties of Holland, England, and America are due.'

IV. Intellectual Activity.

Among the many things said to disparage Calvinism is the statement that it is a relic of an unenlightened and barbarous past; that it is an anachronism in this age of softened and refined civilization. If this be true, then we are confronted with some more of the bishop's 'accidents of history'.

It is a patent fact that Calvinism awoke to life with the revival of learning in Western Europe. Geneva was not more famed as a centre of moral than as a centre of intellectual light. Calvin's renown as an educator was not less than his renown as a religious reformer. His illustrious pupil, John Knox, was the father of the parish school system in Scotland. Bancroft says that 'the Calvinists of Scotland by their system of schools lifted the nation far above any other nation of Europe, excepting, perhaps, some cantons of Switzerland.' This exception only does honour to the Calvinists of Switzerland. Holland in the midst of her desperate struggle for existence founded great institutions of learning; and from Calvinistic Holland and Scotland the public school system was brought to America.

In 1647 it was ordered in all Puritan colonies that every township, after the Lord hath increased them to fifty householders, shall appoint one to teach all children to read and write; and when any town shall increase to the number of one hundred families, they shall set up a grammar school, the masters thereof being able to instruct youth so far as they may be fitted for the university. Sixteen years after the landing of *The Mayflower,* Harvard University was founded, being named for Rev. John Harvard, a young Calvinistic preacher. 'During its first century half its graduates entered the pulpit of Puritanism.' Yale was founded by the Congregational Church, at that time thoroughly Calvinistic. Its first trustees were ten ministers of that denomination. Princeton is the child of Calvinism, being born of the Scotch-Irish Presbyterian Church.

This is rather a surprising accident of history, that a creed, embodying the sentiments and ideas of a dark and savage age, should have quickened an intense thirst for knowledge, and caused its adherents to blaze the way in all civilized countries for both popular and higher education.

It is further strange that it should have been the creed to make the most stringent demands for an educated ministry, even pressing this demand in the case of most Calvinistic churches to the extent of making a high standard of education a *sine qua non* of entering the ministry. The fact is, Calvinism can only live in the light. It was almost suffocated by the gloom of the 'Dark Ages', being represented by only a few of the illustrious names that shine out like stars in the deep darkness of that long night—Anselm, Aquinas, Basil, Bernard, Bede, Wycliffe, Huss. It is the unrelenting foe of ignorance and superstition. It rests not alone on the explicit statements of Scripture, but also on the ascertained laws of the human mind. While it wins the love of the devout heart by its exalted views of God, it at the same time leads captive the profound philosopher by its correct views of man.

V. Spiritual Aggressiveness.

A creed furnishing no incentive to missions for the world's salvation needs nothing else to condemn it. Jesus Christ was above all a missionary, and no church can be imbued with his spirit and not have a zeal for missions.

It is a common accusation against Calvinism that it makes man a passive puppet in the hands of God; that by its doctrine of divine decrees it leaves no motive to human effort. Why should man concern himself about a result which from eternity has been rendered certain by an immutable decree of God?

It would be easy to show that this silly cavil has no force except against a mere caricature of Calvinism. Divine decrees determine no results apart from the divinely appointed means by which results are to be accomplished. Calvinism not only allows scope for the exercise of spiritual energies, but 'the accidents of history', to use Bishop Hurst's convenient phrase, show conclusively that Calvinism stimulates spiritual energy into intense activity.

We do not say that Calvinistic churches have been alone in zeal for missions; nor do we say that they have measured up to the standard of duty; but we do say that Calvinism has been the mightiest spiritual force in the missionary movements of the past century. Calvin, be it said to his lasting credit, sent missionaries to carry the gospel to the heathen in Brazil. This shows the effect of his doctrinal belief on his own heart. Little was done, however, for two hundred years after his death to carry out the Saviour's royal command. The Protestant churches were too busy fighting for the right to live.

William Carey is the recognized father of modern missions to the heathen. He was a sound Calvinist, of Baptist persuasion. From Carey till our day the blue banner of Calvinism has been floating in the very front ranks of the sacramental host who, not counting their lives dear unto themselves, have gone forth to assault the strongholds of Satan in the darkest places of the earth. In addition to Carey, the names of his co-labourers, Marshman and Ward, shed a glory on the English Baptists. To the same church in this country belongs the honour of having enrolled among its missionary heroes the radiant names of Judson and Boardman.

Worthy to be associated with these are the great leaders from other Calvinistic churches, Livingstone, Moffat, McKay, Duff, Wilson, Morrison, and others too numerous to mention. These are mentioned only to show that whatever of glory rests upon Protestant Christendom for the zeal it has manifested in the extension of Christ's kingdom, rests with intensest splendour upon those branches of the church whose creed is supposed by many to paralyze spiritual energy. The Presbyterians of this country, who are the most solidly Calvinistic of any division of the sacramental host, have on their rolls less than one-tenth of the communicants of our land, and more than one-fourth of the foreign missionaries.

Time will not permit us to pursue our investigations further. Are not these fruits, which stand out conspicuously on the surface of modern history, challenging the attention of all men, and winning the admiration of all impartial students, sufficient to demonstrate the quality of the tree? Moral integrity, heroic endurance, an impassioned love for liberty, an ardent thirst for knowledge, and a tireless zeal for missions—surely these are the elements which give beneficent power to a church, and are the credentials of her divine origin. It is frequently asserted that Calvinism is dying. It is to be feared that 'the wish is father to the thought.' Calvinism cannot die.

> Truth crushed to earth will rise again;
> The eternal years of God are hers.

It must struggle against mighty opposition in a world that is so largely dominated by 'the father of lies'; but God is the guarantee of its perpetuity and final triumph. 'Calvinism is the spirit', says Froude,

which rises in revolt against untruth; the spirit which has appeared and re-appeared, and in due time will appear again, unless God is a delusion, and man be as the beasts that perish. For it is but the inflashing upon the conscience of the nature and origin of the laws by which mankind are governed. When all else has failed; when patriotism has covered its face, and human courage has broken down; when intellect has yielded with a smile or a sigh, content to philosophize in the closet, and abroad worship with the vulgar; when emotion, and sentiment, and tender, imaginative piety have become the handmaids of superstition, and have dreamt themselves into forgetfulness that there was any difference between truth and lies, the slavish form of belief called Calvinism has borne an inflexible front to illusion and mendacity, and has preferred rather to be ground to powder, like flint, than to bend before violence or melt under enervating temptation.

———————

OTHER CALVIN TITLES
PUBLISHED BY THE TRUST

SERMONS

Sermons on Genesis 1-11:4, 900pp cloth
Sermons on II Samuel, 696pp cloth
Sermons on Job, 784pp cloth facsimile
Sermons on the Beatitudes, 128pp cloth
*Songs of the Nativity: Selected Sermons on
Luke 1-2,* 280pp cloth
Sermons on Acts 1-7, 688pp cloth
Sermons on Galatians, 688pp cloth
Sermons on Ephesians, 728pp cloth

COMMENTARIES

Genesis, 1088pp cloth
Jeremiah & Lamentations, 5 vols. cloth
Daniel, 808pp cloth
Hosea, 544pp cloth
Joel, Amos & Obadiah, 520pp cloth
Jonah, Micah & Nahum, 544pp cloth
Habakkuk, Zephaniah & Haggai, 416pp cloth
Zechariah & Malachi, 720pp cloth

OTHER TITLES

Tracts and Letters, 7 vols., cloth
Truth for All Time, 156pp soft cover gift edition